Citizen Wealth

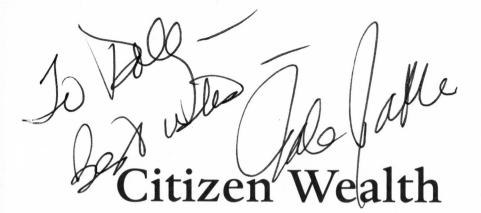

Citizen Wealth

Winning the Campaign to Save Working Families

WADE RATHKE

BK

Berrett–Koehler Publishers, Inc.
San Francisco
a BK Currents book

Berrett-Koehler Publishers, Inc.
235 Montgomery Street, Suite 650
San Francisco, CA 94104-2916
Tel: (415) 288-0260   Fax: (415) 362-2512
www.bkconnection.com

Ordering Information
Quantity sales. Special discounts are available on quantity purchases by corporations, associations, and others. For details, contact the "Special Sales Department" at the Berrett-Koehler address above.
Individual sales. Berrett-Koehler publications are available through most bookstores. They can also be ordered directly from Berrett-Koehler: Tel: (800) 929-2929; Fax: (802) 864-7626; www.bkconnection.com.
Orders for college textbook/course adoption use. Please contact Berrett-Koehler: Tel: (800) 929-2929; Fax: (802) 864-7626.
Orders by U.S. trade bookstores and wholesalers. Please contact Ingram Publisher Services: Tel: (800) 509-4887; Fax: (800) 838-1149; E-mail: customer.service@ingrampublisherservices.com; or visit www.ingrampublisherservices.com / Ordering for details about electronic ordering.

Berrett-Koehler and the BK logo are registered trademarks of Berrett-Koehler Publishers, Inc.

Printed in the United States of America

Berrett-Koehler books are printed on long-lasting acid-free paper. When it is available, we choose paper that has been manufactured by environmentally responsible processes. These may include using trees grown in sustainable forests, incorporating recycled paper, minimizing chlorine in bleaching, or recycling the energy produced at the paper mill.

Library of Congress Cataloging-in-Publication Data

Rathke, Wade.
Citizen wealth: winning the campaign to save working families / by Wade Rathke. – 1st ed.
    p.   cm.
Includes bibliographical references.
ISBN 978-1-57675-862-5 (hardcover : alk. paper)
1. Home ownership – United States. 2. Working class – United States. I. Title.

HD7287.82.U6R38 2009
333.33 80973 – dc22

                    2009008710

First Edition
14 13 12 11 10 09   10 9 8 7 6 5 4 3 2 1

Project management, design, and composition by Steven Hiatt / Hiatt & Dragon, San Francisco
Copyediting: Steven Hiatt   Proofreading: Tom Hassett

To the thousands of community residents and workers
it has been my pleasure to serve, and to
Beth, Chaco, and Diné for sharing my life's love and labor
and this book from cover to cover with me.

Contents

Part III Changing the Terms of the Debate

Preface

I am tired of hard-working families still not being able to make ends meet. I do not believe that people have to be poor.

I do not think I am alone.

I have spent forty years as an organizer doing what I know how to do to help people pull the ends together more tightly. Some days, I think we only have to pull a little harder. Other days, I am not sure the ends will ever join. Somehow, though, rather than becoming completely jaded, I continue to believe that, if they could, a lot of people are like you and me, and would like to do something about the fact that there is way more month than money for most families.

I think the answer is taking the concept of citizen wealth seriously and then working very, very hard to get people to a place where they actually have sufficient citizen wealth. In this book I am going to try and bring you along with me.

By *citizen wealth* I mean the combination of income and assets that provides a family with a measure of real economic security.

Income includes jobs that pay living wages, the power to organize collectively to secure a higher income and better benefits at work, and the ability to access the full range of income maintenance and supports that have been created by various levels of government. Income at a sufficient level guarantees family survival.

Assets, on the other hand, add a level of security to the complex equation of family survival. Assets include savings, access to credit, and, more often than not, decent and affordable housing, including home ownership.

There is more to both income and assets than this simple list, like good healthcare coverage or access to education and training and therefore opportunity, but even progress along these simple lines begins to create real citizen wealth, and therefore real family security, widening the gap between families and potential poverty by miles rather than millimeters. This is a goal worth the work.

I am not naïve, nor do I believe that any of you should be. I think there is little point to building citizen wealth if we do not simultaneously protect what we are building from wholesale erosion. That means that we have to make sure that the wealth being acquired is not immediately dissipated by various predatory practices. We cannot forge ahead two steps toward greater family security and then let down our guard and watch people pushed back again because we did not keep in mind that it all can be taken away in a minute by hundreds of schemes devised for just that purpose.

This work means that some things have to be done better in terms of policy and the politics that drive policy, but this is not a book about policy. At least, it is not a book about just policy.

The work, in my view, really means things that we can do as individuals and communities to create the conditions that allow citizen wealth to become a major priority and thus a visible reality. Since I have been an organizer all of my adult life, much of what I argue, not surprisingly, has to do with collective action and organization. Superman may be able to do everything in the comics, but the rest of us need to join together at every level in order to build the power to do something about these issues. Furthermore, this method works, and I will share with you many examples of campaigns that have succeeded in making a difference in building citizen wealth.

All of this is so important. I wish I were sitting next to you right now and we could hash it out together. I just know that if we talked it through, you would be as moved as I am, and would be rip-roaring and ready to act. That is the organizer in me talking. I have a lot of confidence in those skills and in our ability, yours and mine, to come up with a plan and to make it happen. I am pretty clear about the fact that I am a much better organizer than I am a writer, and this worries me as we start the journey of this book together. I need you to make it through, even if there are rough and imperfect patches, because, as I have said, this is important, and there are things you and I can and should do.

So, bear with me. For my part, I guarantee it will not be boring. I also guarantee that you will learn some things you did not know before you cracked the cover of this book. I know I did.

The Road Ahead

We need to create citizen wealth and ensure the financial security that allows all families to build better lives and better futures, and here is how I have tried to tackle it in this book.

The Introduction, "From the Bottom Up," makes the case that we need to focus on citizen wealth in face of the mounting economic inequities in our society, and explains why I believe my experience as the founder and chief organizer for ACORN (the Association of Community Organizations for Reform Now) for thirty-eight years has taught me, along with a lot of other things, some lessons that are valuable in building citizen wealth.

Chapter 1, "Building a Winning Campaign for Economic Security," looks at the fact that we often fail to think about wealth and concentrate on just income when we think about economic security. Income is important, but assets are important as well because they often define a family's degree of security. These are the differences that can define why a family confronting job loss can suddenly be pushed within a few months from being solidly middle income to being homeless. It all matters.

Chapter 2, "Home Ownership Through Community Reinvestment," deals with home ownership, since the home has become the single biggest asset for working families in the United States. The centrality of increasing home ownership for families of modest means has only increased since the passage of the Community Reinvestment Act in 1977.

Chapter 3, "Stopping Foreclosures and Predatory Lending," looks at how the predatory practices in the subprime mortgage market have eroded family wealth and jeopardized home ownership. We may think we know this story all too well now, but this chapter looks under the hood at the fight to keep home loans flowing to eligible families before the lack of oversight and enforcement drowned many homeowners in foreclosures.

Chapter 4, "Making Work Pay Living Wages," looks at the successful efforts mounted in communities and states throughout the U.S. to increase wages for publicly contracted work and to raise the minimum wage to more adequate levels, despite the lag in the federal minimum wage in recent decades. In this chapter we look at the hard lesson of sometimes putting aside our "dream" goals and focusing realistically on what can win and make a difference.

Chapter 5, "Creating Wealth Through Worker Organizations," takes on an issue that too many people like to avoid. Unions mean much-needed wage and benefit security, yet unions are becoming weaker. In this chapter I argue that we should create more workplace organizations that can enable workers to come together to get the best deals available, and therefore achieve more economic security. Furthermore, in one of the unrecognized success stories of the last thirty years, just such an approach has led to the successful organization of hundreds of thousands of informal workers at the bottom in home health and home day care.

Chapter 6, "Making Earned Income Tax Credits Work for Workers," looks at the Earned Income Tax Credit (EITC), which just about every president and politicians of every stripe claim is the most effective anti-poverty program in the U.S. Despite all of the praise that EITC gets, however, significant numbers of eligible families are not getting EITC benefits, and I argue for an effective campaign to achieve what we call "maximum eligible participation."

Chapter 7, "Guarding Tax Refunds and Combatting High Prices," also takes a look at the dark side of the coin, even as I remain hopeful that the bright side will prevail. This is particularly the case with Refund Anticipation Loans (RALs), which encourage predatory cash advances to desperate families, eroding the very benefits of EITC. I then look at the steps taken by organizations to reform these practices and the great progress being made.

Chapter 8, "The Debt Trap," examines the role of debt in building citizen wealth. Debt of course often undermines citizen wealth, yet people require loans to access educational opportunities and the housing market, and credit cards are a part of our modern economy and can be a form of security for families. We do little in the microfinance area to assist families trying to broaden income opportunities, though, and we need to force established financial institutions to limit credit card abuse and push them to compete with payday lending outfits in providing small loans for low-income families.

Chapter 9, "The 'Maximum Eligible Participation' Solution," argues what I believe should be accepted as a simple truth: if a family is eligible for a benefit, then we need to do everything we can to ensure that that family receives the benefit. We need to finish the jobs that have only been partially done by existing programs at the local, state, and federal level by creating access, doing outreach, and achieving maximum eligible participation.

Part III, "Changing the Terms of the Debate," looks at the ways that both companies and organizations can lead the way to creating citizen wealth by rethinking their markets and constituencies.

Chapter 10, "Working with Corporations to Create an Asset Climate," examines the major steps taken by HSBC to move from being the largest facilitator and financer of RALs to deciding to protect its brand and move out of the market.

Chapter 11, "Business Models That Foster Citizen Wealth," looks at how H&R Block altered its business model to expand wealth for its largely modest-income clientele just as other companies including Wal-Mart and Colonial Penn Insurance had done.

Chapter 12, "Bringing Citizens into the Wealth-Building Process," talks about the potential of bringing diverse partners, from tax preparers (H&R Block) to software firms (Nets to Ladders/N2L) and community-based organizations (ACORN), to work together to create new platforms that combine many programs to achieve greater access and participation.

Chapter 13, "The Future of Citizen Wealth," makes the case that there is a campaign to achieve citizen wealth for working families that needs to be undertaken now and that there is a role for all of us in winning this battle.

As I promised, this will not be boring!

Wade Rathke
New Orleans
March 2009

Introduction

From the Bottom Up

Let us try to sing another song rather than another verse, the same as the first. I am not saying it will be easy, and I may have to catch myself as I fall into the same habits. We have memorized so many of the old verses that, at the first note we hear, it is difficult not to start singing immediately what we already know. However, we need new songs in our future with more hope and promise than those we have seen in the past. We are going to try our hardest to find a way to craft them together, so that we can all march to a different tune.

The acceleration in income inequity over the past several decades is well known and well documented. During the last twenty-five years, the gap between rich and poor has grown almost fivefold.[1] Federal tax giveaways to those in the higher income brackets have not only created shameful disparities, but have also applied additional pressures on future prospects that now must be shed. We have entire cities in the United States, including Boston, Seattle, New York, and Washington, where working families earning moderate incomes can survive only if, like farmers, they owned their land before the boom times and have not lost it in the waves of refinancing and foreclosures now buffeting the economy. This is an epidemic that has resulted in falling health standards, increased mortality, denied educational and other opportunities, depressed wages and incomes, and a score of other conditions unthinkable in a healthy and successful society. In mid-2008, a record number of Americans (more than 80 percent[2]) said that they believed the country was on the wrong track. Rather than being a Cassandra warning of dire consequences to come, I argue that such a course is not inevitable or predetermined, especially if we are willing to alter the paradigm and focus on the ways and means of creating citizen wealth.

I am not an optimist looking through rose-colored glasses; I am in fact quite the opposite.

Having worked as chief organizer for ACORN (Association of Community Organizations for Reform Now)—"first and stayed the longest"—for nearly forty years, I have encountered hundreds of campaigns designed to create citizen wealth, or at least to prevent the erosion of the financial health and well-being of our constituency of low- and moderate-income families. These campaigns have been established both in the United States and around the world.[3] None of this work has been easy, and all of it has met with fierce opposition at every twist and turn. Therefore, I cannot pretend that anything I am going to advocate from our experience or from the experiences of many other organizations is going to be met with open arms, much less with open wallets. Changing the paradigm to winning wealth for our citizens is going to be a process involving some hand-to-hand combat. My goal is to recruit you as a soldier in this new battle with every word you read.

We have to change the narrative in a clear-eyed and hard-fisted way. The Horatio Alger story of our modern Gilded Age spins out constantly in every news cycle. This includes the *People* magazine / *Forbes* 400 versions of the lives of the rich and famous. The outer limits of the absurd gap between rich and poor in the United States are defined by a story on CBS about the status and wealth envy in Manhattan between the mere millionaires and the mega-millionaires.[4] We need little more than the current profound recession, frequently cited as the worst economic situation since the Great Depression, to remind all of us of the thin line between security and deprivation and making a mockery of the stories that were so current only months before the bottom fell out.

Meanwhile, there are 300 million other Americans—and at least 32 percent of the 300 million are low and moderate income.[5] This particular population is, in fact, singing another verse that is the same as the first. These families are being dropped from health insurance coverage at accelerating rates,[6] and they are unable to finance higher education for their children.[7] All of this is taking place as the gains in home ownership over the last decade have been erased overnight,[8] leaving 3 million to 4 million families to face foreclosure.[9] All of these factors contribute to the loss of homes, which is the basis for most definitions of citizen wealth for low- and moderate-income families.[10]

I have traveled a long road to the place where I want to stand with you to fight for citizen wealth. When I was an organizer for the National Welfare Rights Organization (NWRO) in Springfield and Boston, Massachusetts, in the late 1960s, our primary slogan on every sign and banner was ADEQUATE INCOME NOW! Women on welfare did not win then and are certainly not winning now. However, in some ways this unrecognized issue is still at the center of the campaign for citizen wealth. In ACORN we saw something surprising start to happen over the decades. Since we began pitched battles in the mid-1970s against the banks that were exploiting our neighborhoods, we have not only seen the passage of programs that make a difference, like the Community Reinvestment Act (CRA) in 1977,[11] but we have also seen some of our opponents in these campaigns gradually changing course and becoming partners. These new partners have learned that a business model serving low- and moderate-income families rather than avoiding them is not only important to us, but can also be a valuable franchise and major profit center. In fact, the results of these campaigns are significant. In one decade these ACORN campaigns have, estimated conservatively, won $15 billion in direct economic benefits in the form of direct transfers from the government and corporations to lower-income families.[12] This is my definition of creating citizen wealth!

Over the last ten years, ACORN's Financial Justice Center has been able to focus on developing campaigns against the predatory practices of financial institutions, tax preparers, credit card companies, payday lenders, mortgage companies, and servicers (which are mostly no longer banks). During these hard-fought efforts, the Financial Justice Center has found not only that change is possible, but also that it is possible to create a different and better world. I am speaking of a world in which the interests of customers as consumers and constituents can be reconciled to a more comfortable coexistence with corporate America. We have not found that this is a natural impulse. We have noticed, however, that once firms have been forced to adapt they are able to embrace a new future that is compatible with a vision of citizen wealth that is more constructive than corporate banditry.

We want to model good behavior and make the most of the surprising paradox that has emerged from many ACORN campaigns around financial justice and wealth creation. The focus of these campaigns is on governments and corporations that have determinedly resisted initiatives to increase citizen wealth and have then found, to their amazement, that they also benefit from the shift in thinking and new business and service models that reclaim the mission of citizen economic development and improvement as a core pursuit of the American project and promise. Such a premise requires governments to design their citizen wealth programs as a positive good, rather than focusing all their implementation efforts on the negative, obsessed with the rare instances of fraud or error. The public debate on government needs to focus on the increased resources and revenue of a citizenry with greater wealth and on the ability to see "all boats rise" rather than on the usual complaints about small leakage in positive public initiatives in these areas. Similarly, firms need to understand that a wealthier citizenry benefits the bottom line of all enterprises. This is a more constructive and sustainable business model than a constant fleecing of pennies and dollars through hidden and corrosively predatory practices "just because they can." It has been our work for decades to prove that they cannot. I am not arguing that they will inevitably be caught, but that businesses operating within this framework are shortsighted and not even serving their own interests.

Focusing on citizen wealth is neither natural nor easy for any of these outfits. I cannot maintain that this is a wide sweeping trend that is suddenly the rage in corporate boardrooms and in the halls of government. I am arguing quite the opposite. There have been huge struggles for wealth creation and significant successes for tens of thousands of citizens at the bottom that, if expanded and built upon, could revolutionize our society and achieve real and lasting equity—if these paradigms are sufficiently supported and scaled as part of policy, program, and practice.

I also think we have learned some lessons from thousands of campaigns that were created to fight government and some of the world's most prominent corporations both on the streets and at the bargaining tables—in engaging, shaping, and, in some rare cases, changing their operational models and in persuading them to change their political position to advance financial justice by creating citizen wealth. This will lead to increased resources for their own enterprises, whether private or public. My argument is that, just maybe, this is possible and that, perhaps, now is the time to make it happen.

The topic of citizen wealth has become surprisingly controversial in present-day America. Therefore, we must clear that up at the outset, because citizenship itself has become fraught with controversy, when it is really the subject of wealth that should be more the rage. Few seem as exercised as they need to be about wealth, but the notion of "citizen" has been and remains controversial. When I speak of "citizen," I am not projecting the classical Greek view that some would now adopt. The Greeks saw democracy as a radical concept, but it was strictly limited to those who were the sons and daughters of other citizens in places like Athens. Over the years it became harder and harder to become a citizen, and in fact in the 5th century the Athenians removed 5,000 people from the list of citizens to limit those who might be eligible to receive rations from a gift of grain from an Egyptian king.[13] Even then, it seems, where there was a question of wealth versus citizenship, it was clear which would take the hindmost. My use of the term *citizen wealth* throughout this volume is declared in the broadest, most comprehensive, and inclusive sense in the way that the French after the 14th century defined a citizen as being any "inhabitant of the country." After the French Revolution, the common greeting on the street from one person in France to another was "Citizen ...," in the same way we might say "Mr.," "Ms," or "Brother," or as South Africans say and Russians once said, "Comrade." This signified that we were all together in making the revolution and trying to build one united, if not always happy, family. I will be speaking about citizen wealth in this all-encompassing way, because our vision here is to see all lower-income and working families moving further away from poverty, and I draw no distinctions there, and require no fingerprints or picture identification. If you inhabitant this country, then I want to imagine our creating plans and programs that find all citizens ahead and none left behind.

I hope to prove, with your help, that there should be a different paradigm, and that perhaps together, using your personal methods and keeping me in mind, we can force the pieces to fit more closely and smoothly together to create real citizen wealth.

Let us see if we can get there together.

Part I
Creating Citizen Wealth

1

Building a Winning Campaign for Economic Security

The Bible may have assured some people that the poor would always be with us, but there is no support in Scripture for the view that their numbers must necessarily be as huge as they are today. We should instead believe that poverty is a relative concept, meaning that some families are relatively poor compared to those who are rich, rather than an absolute concept, meaning that some families are sentenced by circumstance, fate, or fortune to the most abject levels of deprivation and poverty.

The task of making sense of all of this can be daunting. Every morning's headlines seem to carry the subtext these days that economics is about as much a science as astrology. The basic strategy seems to be to throw as much money against the wall as can be printed and hope that it sticks long enough to prevent the deluge. Managing the economy in these times seems to be driven by hopes and prayers more than anything else. Suffice it to say, all of these issues become very complex when it comes to money, who has too little of it, and how to make sure they have more.

These are problems that arise when we fail to recognize the fact that income alone does not guarantee economic security, nor does income by itself define wealth. In working to advance citizen wealth we need to look closely at how these factors differ and how we can devise strategies or campaigns to create programs that increase not only income, but wealth as well.

This is a big-stakes proposition, and there need to be a lot of players at this table putting actual investments into the pot, not just wild bets. The government is part of the solution here, but so are businesses that depend on lower- and moderate-income families for their success. I also believe there are roles for all of us to play, particularly as recession forces us to confront the fragility of family economic security. We may not be economists, but more and more of us are going to know families who are losing their security, losing their homes, seeing their children come home from colleges they are no longer able to afford, dealing with mature workers finding careers and good jobs suddenly gone. In fact, more and more of us *are* these families, and some of us have been these families for a long time. We have to sort this out.

Low- and Moderate-Income Families

The demographic population that ACORN sees as its primary constituency is low- and moderate-income (LMI) families. Roughly speaking, this "majority constituency" (which includes the 47 percent of American families making less than $50,000 annually; the 21 percent earning between $51,000 and $75,000; and the 14 percent earning between $76,000 and $100,000) adds up to 57 million families in America.[1] This same block of people around the world is obviously an even larger percentage of the population, because the developing world is overflowing with families who are barely surviving. Estimates indicate that a quarter of the world's population makes less than US$2 per day—over 1 billion people![2] At home or abroad, the reality continues to be that there are more people for whom money is a constant, daily concern than there are people who have found a livelihood and income stream that puts them beyond the ravages of want.

Business Models

Firms see such numbers as markets, and they make their own assessments of whether these are customers they want to seek or avoid. Current developments in India around modifications of foreign direct investment in retail, banking, and insurance are interesting because they reveal some of the choices and aspirations of global corporations. In a country of 1.1 billion people, some 300 million in India's emerging middle class are reshaping the market so that global concerns like big-box retail or global financial institutions like Citibank or HSBC can export their brands to such "solid" citizens.

Even so, in the United States some of the same companies see low- and moderate-income families as primary markets for their core businesses. Two good examples in different markets are Wal-Mart and H&R Block. Wal-Mart has succeeded over the last fifty years in building the largest corporation in the United States, with gross sales of some $270 billion and more than two million employees, making it the largest employer by far in the U.S., by using a business model that focuses on full-service retail sales to families making less than $50,000 per year.[3] Kmart and Target like to see themselves as slightly more upscale, but their target customers are still in the solid range of LMI consumers. H&R Block, which specializes in tax services as its core business, focuses its business model on a "preparer dependent" customer who keeps coming back tax season after tax season. Block prepares 20 million tax returns every year, specializing in low- and moderate-income communities, as ACORN discovered in our campaign against some of Block's practices. In fact, H&R Block recently shared with us an internal report indicating that approximately 7 million of its tax-return customers seem to be eligible for any number of federal income support programs, which illustrates the full reach of Block's market penetration among lower-income families.

Certainly these are not the only large companies to specialize in lower-income consumers. The list is in fact a long one, and parts of it are anything but pretty. Cigarette, beer, and liquor companies have long been mainstays in this area. Pawnshops and quick-loan storefronts can be found in virtually any lower-income area, but many have been replaced by the check-cashing and payday loan outfits that have become ubiquitous in lower-income communities. Look within a short radius of Wal-Marts virtually anywhere in the country, including some moderate-income neighborhoods, and you will see not only the check-cashing and payday loan storefronts in nearby strip malls, but also H&R Block, Jackson Hewitt, Liberty, or some local "mom-and-pop" tax place. There will, of course, be fast-food outlets of all shapes and varieties. Increasingly there may not be supermarkets. You may find specialized outlets catering to particular ethnic groups. There will be coin-operated laundromats, liquor stores, bars, churches, daycare centers, rent-a-center or cheap furniture stores, a lot more tire and mechanics' shops to keep beat-up cars hauling their owners to work with bailing wire and chewing gum, used car dealers, and on and on. Many of them are not large national firms, though a surprising number of establishments, like the predatory check-cashing and payday loan boutiques, are supported by the largest and best-known finance houses in the country.

The simple truth is that despite the poverty of many of these communities there are already significant assets embedded there. Recognition of this fact helped drive passage of the Community Reinvestment Act in 1977. Banks were collecting substantial deposits from thousands of individual accounts in poor communities, and the numbers added up to significant proportions of bank assets. But not much of this money returned in the form of loans by the banks back to the local communities where they so readily accepted deposits and held resources.[4]

In fact, the heart of the economics of redlining could be found in the expropriation of these deposited dollars from poorer areas and their transfer to "safer" areas, which were also richer and whiter, to finance home mortgages and similar loans. There were assets, lots of assets, but they were not being allowed to multiply on behalf of their owners, particularly in creating home ownership opportunities or in allowing investments in existing homes that would increase in value. Banks were essentially controlling assets providing their owners minimal to nonexistent returns in order to maximize bank income from higher interest rates and to make supposedly more secure investments outside the community.

Over the last thirty years there has been great progress in reducing redlining, though even now only about 30 percent of the mortgage lenders fall under CRA regulatory requirements for community lending or the Home Mortgage Disclosure Act (HMDA) for reporting on such lending.[5] In the last three decades this area has, despite the CRA, become an unregulated "no man's land."

Part of the business model of many financial institutions over the same period has been to move away from serving individual depositors. It would seem obvious for me now to list banks as another one of the institutions that are firmly rooted in lower-income communities. In fact, it would seem obvious to report that there is great progress in narrowing the gap of the "unbanked" among American lower-income families. Unfortunately, this still does not seem to be the case. Currently, 9 percent of families do not have a bank account.[6] Twenty years ago, 15 percent of families did not have bank accounts.[7] That is not as much progress as we need, and therefore creates a problem experienced routinely in the development of citizen wealth.

Western Union, for example, and new competitors such as Money-Gram and those that offer debit card–based products, are entrenched in lower-income communities, particularly in those with high percentages of immigrant workers and residents, because these companies specialize in handling the transfer of remittances from the U.S. back to the families' home countries. These remittances are now a fundamental component of the national economies of countries throughout the developing world in Africa, Latin America, and Asia.

The Nexus of Wealth

Before we go too far down this path, it is important to understand that most of these business models are focused on capturing income from LMI families, rather than wealth, and therein lies both the problem and the potential lie. At the threshold of our journey, we have to confront a huge problem for people, politicians, and policy. There is a world of difference between income and wealth, and inequities have been increasing in America even more dramatically around wealth than around income.

In "The Hidden Cost of Being African American" Thomas Shapiro makes this point forcefully: "The average American family uses income for food, shelter, clothing, and other necessities. Wealth is different, and ... it is used differently than income. Wealth is what families own, a storehouse of resources. Wealth signifies command over financial resources that when combined with income can produce the opportunity to secure the 'good life' in whatever form is needed—education, business, training, justice, health, comfort, and so on. In this sense wealth is a special form of money not usually used to purchase milk and shoes or other life necessities. More often it is used to create opportunities, secure a desired status and standard of living, or pass class status along to one's children."[8]

Put another way, there are big reasons why the rich are different from the rest of us, and those differences lie right at the nexus of wealth: they can live with a level of security and a variety of opportunities that can only be imagined by the vast majority of working families.

Many make the argument that some progress has been made in reducing income inequality. The income-based U.S. poverty rate was 15.2 percent in 1983 and dropped dramatically to 12.8 percent during the six-year period to 1989, and fell less significantly down to 11.7 percent by 2001.[9] Unfortunately, as important as reducing income equality is, there seems to be a weak correlation between income and wealth. Sociologist Lisa Keister makes this point in her study *Wealth in America*: by focusing "solely on income [we] miss a large part of the story of advantage and disadvantage in America."[10]

The same point is made about the relationships among income, earnings, and wealth by Javier Díaz-Giménez, Vincenzo Quadrini, and José-Victor Ríos-Rull: "Labor earnings, income, and wealth are all unequally distributed among U.S. households, but the distributions are significantly different. Wealth is much more concentrated than the other two. Wealth is positively correlated with earnings and income, but not strongly. The movement of households up and down the economic scale is greater when measured by income than by earnings or wealth. Differences among the three variables remain when the data is disaggregated by age, employment status, educational level, and marital status of heads of U.S. households."[11] All of this seems to be the equivalent for the body politic of getting pneumonia under control and then having to explain to the family that the patient still died because there was no remedy for the cancer.

Since we are now wallowing somewhere between bad news and hard facts, let's consider sociologist Mark Rank's point that to recognize the "true nature of poverty" we "should be looking at American families that experience at least one year of poverty."[12] Rank emphasizes that almost 60 percent of Americans will spend one year below the official poverty line—I can tell you now that organizers will spend more than one, along with many of our members—and that 90 percent of African American families will have this experience during their most productive working years.[13]

Thomas Shapiro also cites the asset poverty line (APL) as helpful in looking at this problem. It's a calculation of the resources needed by a family to survive a crisis period during which they have no income. Suppose, Shapiro argues, that the APL were tied to the official poverty level and we arbitrarily defined a family's crisis period as three months with zero income: "In 1999 the official U.S. government poverty line for a family of four stood at $1,392 a month. In order to live at that poverty line for three months, a family of four needs a safety net of at least $4,175. Families with less than $4,175 in net financial assets in 1999, then, are 'asset-poor.'"[14] It is this kind of calculation that underlies the fear of losing a job or missing a paycheck for a month or two, and marks the difference between family security and homelessness. It is wealth rather than income that provides the safety net for working families, and there simply is not enough wealth and not enough being done to increase it.

It goes without saying that wealth is not color-blind, either. In a 1999 study a little more than a quarter of all white children were raised in such asset-poor families, while 52 percent of African American children were raised that way and 54 percent of Hispanic kids. For whites since 1984 that level has been largely unchanged, while the percentage of blacks has fallen from 67 percent in 1984 and Hispanics have seen increases in asset deprivation.[15]

Most of the business models we looked at earlier focused on how to divert pieces of the income stream of lower-income families to business enterprises. Such income diversions virtually by definition go toward necessities or "survival" items like food, shelter, clothing, fuel, transportation, and health. The Wal-Marts of the world can maintain their hold on the incomes of working families because they specialize in many of these areas. Many other companies contend for this income stream, including other grocery and drugstore operations, car manufacturers, insurance companies, trade schools and community colleges, gas stations, home and rental companies, and so forth through all the categories of consumer and durable products. In many cases, such firms' best-case argument for creating value is similar to Wal-Mart's claims that it saves the working family money and perhaps thereby helps to create wealth.

If we define wealth as based on the resources a family controls and that can be increased by new opportunities, then arguably wealth can be built by deeper training in marketable skills, through education that not only broadens opportunity but also extends social and job networks; by ownership of housing and other property; and by holding savings and other investments. With this being said, where are the companies that see their business model as increasing citizen wealth? The citizen wealth crisis is most dramatically revealed in the current loss of wealth caused by the bait-and-switch methods that were endemic to subprime lending. The financial institutions that supported the subprime system are to blame for the loss of millions of family homes to foreclosure and for the fate of millions of families who are "under water" on the value of their homes compared to the size of their mortgages. All of these families are losing wealth.

Are there companies that have tied their futures to the ability of working families to increase their wealth? Who are they? What are they doing? Why aren't there more of them?

Let's not just pick on corporations, though. There are big stakes here worth billions. Are there any public policies that seek to increase wealth for lower-income families and to help them build some measure of financial security? What are they? How can programs designed to increase income become more connected to the creation of wealth as well?

While we are looking at all of these issues and the importance of wealth, and even as we confront the significant problem that income and wealth are not naturally and organically connected, in the sense that increasing one will automatically raise the other, we still have to acknowledge that the chicken-and-egg problem for families is clear. The problem of what I will call "wealth security" for working families may not be automatically tied to income increases, but it is hard to imagine how we get there from here without significant increases in incomes and, just as important, protections for that income.

If income and earnings are going up, citizen wealth must be leaking away for one of two kinds of reasons. Either the prices of necessities are rising just as rapidly and sucking up the increased income—and a lot of that is no doubt happening, particularly in the costs of food, fuel, and transportation—or there is a direct, predatory siphoning of real income and potential wealth from working families. Increasing citizen wealth requires campaigns to win public policies to maximize the conversion of increased income into citizen wealth and programs to prevent predatory business models that siphon off income and block wealth security and to punish the predators. Both sides of the ledger are important because the stakes are high and the numbers are staggeringly large.

In this fight for family survival, benefits are as important as income in increasing wealth. Health insurance and pensions or other retirement-related benefits are obvious examples, and once again they work because they both create and protect wealth.

A widely recognized fact of life for working families in America these days is the tenuousness of wealth security in the face of a family health crisis. The numbers of Americans covered by health insurance have steeply declined in recent decades to the point now where 14.5 percent of the U.S. population does not have coverage.[16] This assault on income centers on costs and deductibles that leverage income from the family. The attack on wealth is the cascading impact of any health crisis for the uninsured, which has made health crises one of the primary drivers for home foreclosures for many families and for bankruptcies for others, and has made the need to reform healthcare coverage and costs one of the major national political and policy issues of this decade. The math is simple. With full individual or family health coverage there may be an income dislocation as copays and deductibles strain available cash reserves, but a working family that does not qualify for federal health programs like Medicaid and Medicare has definitely lost any paddle and is heading over the falls and down the stream. Citizen wealth cannot be created on the long-shot gamble of good genes and perfect health.

Pensions pose the same challenge. The corporate abrogation of their social contract with workers has led to constant hand-wringing about the Social Security system, of course, but also to cuts in health insurance coverage that have been accompanied by reductions in retirement and pension-related benefits. IRAs and pension accounts are important indexes of wealth and are critically important for protecting security when working years are over and income zeros out. Having or not having income in your nonworking years marks a great divide between the security of citizen wealth and potential abject poverty.

In the big-stakes fight for citizen wealth, the war on benefits continues to punish lower-income families, because benefits have too often become theoretical: they are difficult if not impossible to access and therefore provide no real assistance or security. The trench warfare around eligibility for benefits versus real access to benefits has been too often ideologically driven, rather than factually based and value-free. What is the point of something like food stamps if you cannot get them when you need them, or the point of unemployment, or of any number of similar income and security programs?

We need to create a national economic and political consensus that increasing family income, wealth, and assets is not welfare or an entitlement "giveaway" program but an investment in the public good. We need to win and then to implement programs that create a government and business climate that is family friendly and focuses on increasing citizen well-being and the creation of social and public goods and, as a central part of that focus, on increasing citizen wealth. We cannot ensure the health of our democracy without substituting a wide-ranging effort to create more citizen wealth and benefits for the current dominant political and business models that embrace only caveat emptor or the survival of the fittest.

2

Home Ownership Through Community Reinvestment

For lower-income families, the question of whether or not they hold any citizen wealth at all often begins and ends at the front door.

Among low-income homeowners with household incomes pegged at less than $20,000 per year, 72 percent of their wealth derives from home equity. For lower-income families with incomes between $20,000 and $50,000 per year, home equity accounts for 55 percent of total wealth.[1] For those who rent, the "median wealth of a low-income family is one-twelfth of that of a low-income homeowner."[2]

That divide is huge, making home ownership for lower-income families a critical builder of citizen wealth, and making home retention against the threats of foreclosure an essential component of their economic security.

Nothing about home ownership has happened magically, or because of the "invisible hand" of private enterprise and the home construction and real estate interests.[3] Federal and public policy drove this bus to the front door of millions of houses. This policy thrust started with the creation of Fannie Mae (the Federal National Mortgage Association) in 1938, which operates as a secondary market to capitalize home purchases off the ledger sheets of the banking industry. In addition, the G.I. Bill, passed in 1944, provided special assistance to returning veterans to buy homes, often with Veterans Administration loan guarantees. The drive to increase the rate of home ownership continued with the creation of Freddie Mac (the Federal Home Loan Mortgage

Corporation) in 1970. In 1940, only about 44 percent of Americans owned their own homes. The figure has recently risen as high as 69 percent and is still holding in the mid 60 percent range.

The Community Reinvestment Act

In the last thirty years, the great story of building community wealth has been the fight to win equitable rights to home ownership for minorities. As we shall see, there are still many chapters left to write in this tale, but it all starts with the fight that led first to the passage of the Community Reinvestment Act (CRA) in 1977, and then to the long campaign for the act's implementation. The CRA was passed to deal with a very real problem: entire neighborhoods, usually minority areas of lower-income and working families, were essentially "redlined," meaning that banks refused to lend in these areas and therefore spurred full-scale disinvestment in many inner-city neighborhoods.

None of these effects happened by accident, particularly racial discrimination. The Federal Housing Administration, as a matter of policy, made it clear that segregation was required to maintain housing values, arguing that "if a neighborhood is to retain stability, it is necessary that properties shall continue to be occupied by the same social and racial classes. A change in social or racial occupancy generally contributes to instability and a decline in values."[4]

I well remember the "Save the City" organizing drives initiated by ACORN in Little Rock in 1972, a difficult campaign centered on the Oak Forest neighborhood at what was then the east–west borderline between working neighborhoods and more middle-class and upper-income areas to the west across University Avenue. Oak Forest was majority white at that time, and the organizing committee suddenly found that the only subject people wanted to talk about, a concern echoed loudly at house after house, was the onslaught of scurrilous real estate agents who were trying to "blockbust" the neighborhood by creating a wave of panic selling. Their method was deadly and efficient. Working families had almost all their resources tied up in these tidy little bungalows in Oak Forest. They were being told that black families had just bought into the area on this block or that block, and that if they did not list their houses for sale immediately they were going to be stuck riding the value of their houses down to dirt as the neighborhood became increasingly black. We fought back furiously.

ACORN signs that said "This House Is NOT For Sale" went up everywhere in Oak Forest. We enlisted Carroll O'Connor (Archie Bunker on television), Ryan O'Neal, and Jack Nicholson to do radio public service announcements letting people know that "blockbusting" was against the law thanks to the Fair Housing Act of 1968, passed just a few years before, that banned discrimination in housing based on race, color, religion, or national origin (and later sex, familial status, and disability). In the case of Oak Forest, you can still visit the neighborhood more than a generation later and be impressed with its stability and the fact that there still remains some measure of diversity. Unfortunately, such real estate wars are ones of attrition that many communities cannot win.

The fight to get Congress to pass the Community Reinvestment Act ran much along the lines of the Oak Forest effort. As citizen and community organizations focused on rebuilding the urban core and creating stronger neighborhoods in the inner city, the programs that had fueled redevelopment and investment in the 1960s (for example, Model Cities and the Office of Economic Opportunity) were largely gone or exhausted. The Nixon administration's shift of aid dollars to Community Development Block Grants meant that less money was available from federal sources, and communities in the future would depend on their ability to leverage private dollars into recovery and development. The refusal of banks to participate based on the perceived credit risks of lending to lower-income and racially diverse families meant that without that leverage our neighborhoods were caught in a cycle of decline.

Community groups of various persuasions, such as ACORN, the National Tenant Information Center (NTIC) and its feisty leader, Gail Cincotta of Chicago, NTIC organzer Shel Trapp, and policy experts from the Center for Community Change and other think-tanks and advocacy groups tried to navigate our way around Washington like immigrants in a foreign land, with few resources and little D.C. savvy or capacity. The critical tactical breakthrough came with the passage of the Home Mortgage Disclosure Act of 1975, which spelled the beginning of the end for bank redlining practices, because now we would be able to prove that banks were disproportionately receiving deposits from lower-income and minority communities while investing poor people's money in safer investments in richer areas while refusing to make even minimal loans in the redlined areas. Congressional legislation is a lesson in compromise rather than in crafting perfect public policy. Language embedded in the act that banks involved in community reinvestment could not go beyond "safe and sound" banking operations meant that the seeds of the CRA's undoing were planted in the original legislation. Nonetheless, this was an unprecedented victory for community groups in fighting to build citizen wealth and has continued to be the gold standard for what can be achieved through concerted work, strong coalitions, active demands and demonstrations, effective legislative alliances, and determined lobbying.

As hard as CRA was to enact, the corresponding challenge was to implement the full spirit of the CRA and make it work for urban communities, and this meant the kind of hand-to-hand combat from city to city that an organization like ACORN specialized in undertaking. The two most significant cases that showed both the gains possible from CRA and the act's limits were brought by ACORN and led to Federal Reserve Bank hearings, the first involving Boatman's Bank in St. Louis and the second involving Hibernia National Bank (now CapitalOne) in New Orleans.

Thirty years after passage of the CRA there still have been very few Federal Reserve Bank hearings into lending practices, but the Boatman's Bank hearings were the first, coming fairly quickly after passage of CRA. The bank's name alone seems to evoke memories of a lost, almost quaint, era of community banking in America. Quick research done by ACORN showed that there was nothing quaint about the failure of Boatman's to lend in low-income neighborhoods throughout St. Louis, and this was at a time when the city's neighborhoods were not just migrating from the river to the suburban counties but were galloping away to depopulate the city. ACORN protested the merger within the comment period, and in a precedent-setting move the Federal Reserve Bank of St. Louis agreed to hold a hearing.

The prospect of a Federal Reserve hearing convinced Boatman's to negotiate with ACORN representatives. The agreement that followed was groundbreaking for both ACORN and its future, especially in creating citizen wealth, as well as proving to community groups throughout the country that CRA, for all of its blemishes, offered organizers the leverage they needed for successful campaigns. The delays that could come with CRA hearings meant that the higher cost of delayed transactions, particularly in the 1970s when interest rates were rising dramatically, could alter the entire economics of a deal. Additionally, in the consumer deposit–driven era of community banking in the 1970s, issues of reputation were also critical, and there was no way to avoid the fact that a Federal Reserve hearing gave real legitimacy to ACORN charges that there was de facto discrimination at work in a bank's lending (or nonlending, to be more accurate) policies.

The negotiations led to the creation of a $50 million loan commitment to St. Louis neighborhoods and the establishment of a review committee to oversee the investments. Both ACORN and Boatman's wisely embraced the agreement. A Boatman's spokesperson at the time said, "We're being held up as the heroes, and that's super. That's the kind of publicity we love. And we're not making any loans we feel are bad." An evaluation of this program done several years after the Boatman's campaign by the *St. Louis Post-Dispatch* indicated that the bank had followed through on its commitment, making more than 5,000 loans to new homeowners in the first several years of the commitment.

The fight with Hibernia was more difficult and actually went through a full-blown hearing at the offices of the Federal Reserve Bank on Poydras Avenue in New Orleans. ACORN had less leverage in this case because we were challenging Hibernia's purchase of a smaller bank in Louisiana, a bank that was very conservative and "southern" to its core in the insulated way that has been common to New Orleans businesses. Nevertheless, ACORN proved its charges against the bank in its complaint. The Office of the Controller of the Currency (OCC) had rated Hibernia as "satisfactory" on its CRA performance, but when the Federal Reserve Board investigated it found the bank's performance "woefully inadequate" without even "proper records to support an evaluation."[5] The Federal Reserve Board did end up approving the Hibernia acquisition, but it did so on the condition that Hibernia develop and submit a plan to improve its performance under CRA, which ACORN felt at the time was a victory.

Perhaps more significantly, the Fed indicated that no new petitions from Hibernia would be approved without "substantive improvements." Unfortunately, the Fed would not release any documentation of Hibernia's improvements to ACORN as a matter of its cozy confidentiality policy in relation to supervised banks. We later learned to our chagrin that Hibernia had in fact failed to submit any documents, and to make matters worse, several future Hibernia petitions were approved despite Hibernia's noncompliance with the Fed's ruling.[6] The result was an unfortunate harbinger of the future, since it revealed a "catastrophic failure in the enforcement of the CRA" without any real policy changes benefiting low- and moderate-income communities.[7]

Agreements like the ones forged by ACORN with Boatman's Bank have been duplicated over and over around the country with the emergence of interstate banking and the array of mergers resulting in larger and larger money center banks or superbanks. This wave of bank consolidation has been a mixed blessing. The existence of fewer small community banks means that it is harder to create tailored agreements more closely fitting specific needs in distinct communities. On the other hand, ACORN's agreements with larger institutions have over time become deep, multifaceted partnerships funded in the millions, committing and delivering literally billions of dollars' worth of home mortgage money to impacted low- and moderate-income neighborhoods. ACORN's partnerships with Citibank, Bank of America, JPMorgan Chase, and others have created the resources allowing ACORN's sister organization, the ACORN Housing Corporation (AHC), to devise a loan counseling program for lower-income families focusing on more than thirty ACORN cities. Over the post-CRA decades, hundreds of thousands of our members and neighborhood residents in these cities have moved into first-time home ownership.

The impact of CRA has had the desired effect of significantly increasing the home ownership percentages of minority households and therefore of creating huge amounts of bottom-line citizen wealth. For example, by mid-1997 (twenty years after the passage of CRA) according to Controller of the Currency Eugene Ludwig (the principal regulator of the nation's largest banks), "CRA agreements had produced total commitments for over $215 billion of increased loans and investments in underserved areas."[8]

The rough math gives a sense of proportion and suggests the scale of what community groups and community coalitions were able to create in commitments over the first twenty years of CRA. Let's look at Ludwig's estimate of $215 billion in CRA agreements. If we estimate that the average price of a home in lower-income neighborhoods was $100,000, we get some perspective on the achievements of the high-pressure campaigns that created such achievements at the bargaining table. The number of homes moved to ownership through these agreements alone, according to this simple math, would be 2,150,000—more than 2 million houses in less than twenty years. This figure, added to a reasonable estimate that the number of agreements in the next ten-year period would be at least equal to those in the previous ten years, meant that there would be another $108 billion in such CRA agreements. That would translate into 1,080,000 homes leveraged into the hands of lower-income and working families, for a total of more than 3.2 million homes in our communities. It is harder to estimate what may have been the shift in banking patterns outside the parameters of these agreements. Even if the amount driven simply by the legislation and "safe and sound" banking practices were only equal to what emerged from the table, that would yield another 2 million to 3 million homes. A combined total of more than 6 million over the thirty years would be mind-boggling.

Is this possible? Perhaps, and in fact it is likely that these numbers are shockingly modest. Annual loans to African Americans tripled in the four-year period 1991–95, from 45,000 to 138,000, a half-million loans in just that one span, while loans to Hispanics more than doubled.[9]

In the period 1994–2001, the annual home ownership rate for all minorities rose from 43.2 percent to 49.0 percent. In absolute numbers, that meant that the number of minority homeowners in the period spiked from 9.5 million to 13.3 million, an increase of 3.8 million.[10] In June 2002, President George W. Bush announced that he wanted to narrow the gap between minority and white home ownership by creating programs that would put 5.5 million minority households into home ownership by 2010. In short, an increase in 5 million homes resulting strictly from the passage of CRA in all likelihood drastically understates the enormity of this achievement.

This coupling of race and inequity has been an intractable issue, though, so we cannot pat ourselves on the back and relax, having checked a box somewhere, one problem solved and on to the next. The gap between white and nonwhite home ownership, and therefore in many ways in wealth itself, remains significant. In 2002, according to the U.S. Census Bureau, the home ownership rate for white households was 74.2 percent, with virtually three of every four white families being homeowners. For African Americans and Hispanic households, it was closer to one out of every two, with 47.1 percent and 47.2 percent, respectively, being homeowners. Asians and other races fared a little better, at 55.8 percent home ownership.

The CRA has thus been among the most significant engines of wealth growth for lower-income families over the last thirty years. However, the racial/ethnic home ownership gap remains, and, perhaps as important, the CRA itself has become less and less effective in its ability to leverage reductions in the ownership gap. Banks are now the caboose on the mortgage lending train, rather than the locomotive pulling the load as they were thirty years ago. Estimates are that less than 30 percent of mortgage lending institutions are now covered by CRA requirements and reporting,[11] although this number is changing rapidly as financial institutions in the current meltdown reorganize as bank holding companies to qualify for bailout monies and now find themselves under the CRA.

More amazingly to community groups that have been so intimately involved with the implementation of CRA, and despite abundant studies indicating that CRA lending has been hugely profitable,[12] the actual enforcement of CRA by the Federal Reserve and the Office of the Controller of the Currency has often been pathetic,[13] and Congress has diluted the requirements every decade. Mortgage companies are not covered by CRA requirements, yet until recently they have made the majority of mortgage loans. Despite the fact that various studies have shown that mortgage companies direct a relatively small percentage of their loans to disadvantaged areas, such companies continue to be able to sell the loans to Fannie Mae and Freddie Mac. These loans come with all of the government guarantees involved in such secure transactions but without any requirement to meet the needs of communities. Not surprisingly, this sets the stage for abuses without addressing systemic wealth problems in these communities or among impacted populations.

There are also some lenders outside the coverage of CRA that are still involved in some form of redlining. Secondary mortgage markets and private mortgage insurers, for example, "will not buy loans for properties on blocks with more than 15 percent abandonment,"[14] and other institutions have required high-percentage down payments on the total purchase price for housing for lower-income families with some credit constraints.[15] Overreliance on Fair Isaacs Credit (FICA) scores is not the same as redlining, but disqualifying lower-income families based on FICA scores can have the same impacts on both citizen wealth and community stability, as we will explore later in this book.

The other side of the coin in looking at the gap in minority home ownership is not simply racial discrimination in lending. It is the increasingly intractable problem of income and age differences and how they reflect home ownership patterns. The American Housing Survey of 2001 was color-blind and indicated that rates of home ownership also followed income: 45.7 percent home ownership for families making less than $10,000 a year, 53.5 percent for those between $10,000 and $25,000, 64.2 percent for those between $25,000 and $50,000, 82.5 percent for those between $50,000 and $100,000, and 92.1 percent for those making over $100,000 per year.[16] Simply put, if a family is making it, they own it, and if they don't own it, they aren't making it. Something of the same is true for age, though the effect is not as dramatic. The U.S. Census Bureau reports that 42.7 percent of those under age thirty-five were homeowners, 69 percent for those between thirty-five and forty-four, 77.2 percent of those between forty-five and fifty-four, 81.3 percent between fifty-five and sixty-four, and 80.8 percent aged sixty-five and over.[17]

Intergenerational Wealth

Since we are now wallowing around on the dark side of this problem, we ought to also consider these very gaps at the nexus of home ownership as one of the primary generators of wealth for lower-income families. These gaps, along with barriers imposed by income differences that are also systemic and historic, as well as the problems of younger families and households, also lead to the huge and persistent stratification of citizen wealth. This is because such factors affect the intergenerational transfer of wealth, or more plainly, the lack of such transfers.

Wealth, much more than the sins of the fathers, is passed down from generation to generation. The ability or inability of a family to maneuver its way into home ownership and hang on to any kind of higher-paying job means that future generations are forced to continue to climb the ladder rung by rung, which is the hardest way to get up from the bottom of the citizen wealth pile.

A powerful study by the Joint Center for Housing Studies at Harvard found that intergenerational wealth was also directly tied to housing. "Not only does homeownership provide access to housing wealth, but it also has indirect impacts that are crucial for low-income households. Specifically, parental homeownership indirectly impacts child labor earnings through increased educational attainment ... and children from owner-occupied households have fewer social problems, which also seems to augment labor earnings."[18]

In order to facilitate intergenerational wealth, hanging on to a home is job number one for many lower-income families, and that is a special challenge in these times.

Immigrants and Home Ownership

Immigrants as well as citizens own homes, and according to a 2001 study on home ownership by Georgetown University's Institute for the Study of International Migration, immigrants are three times as likely to value home ownership as their native-born counterparts,[19] and yet only 49 percent of America's foreign-born population actually owns a home, as opposed to 74 percent of native nonminority Americans.[20]

Banks have been on the cutting edge in developing the home mortgage market among immigrants, regardless of documentation, some quietly and some publicly. As a result of negotiations with both Bank of America and Citibank, ACORN and its affiliate ACORN Housing were able to launch huge programs through our housing counseling services where mortgages were approved based on federal Individual Taxpayer Identification Numbers (ITINs) rather than any other form of identification. Both institutions were highly publicity adverse about these programs even as they embraced the results enthusiastically, since at the time ITIN loan closings were flying out of their offices, particularly in California and Texas home markets. Smaller banks, though, were much more open in their advertising and outreach, particularly in heavily Latino markets, and developed profitable lending niches in these areas.

Our interest may be citizen wealth, but banks were concentrating fully on the bottom line, and the regulators were not simply giving them a "pass," they were giving them the high sign. "Banks are not an arm of the immigration department," noted Kevin Mukri, a spokesperson for the Office of the Comptroller of the Currency, the primary bank regulator. "As long as those getting mortgages meet the requirements of being authorized bank customers, including proper ID, it would be discriminatory not to service them."[21] And, to put a fine point on it, trade publication *U.S. Banker* happily added, "There is no law against banks issuing mortgages to illegal immigrants, nor against their owning property in the U.S."[22] The same piece also found additional justification for the program from the Federal Deposit Insurance Corporation (FDIC). Its spokesman, Michael Frias, helpfully confirmed that "there is no federal banking law that requires banks to verify the immigration status of foreign account holders."[23] Mortgage Guaranty Insurance Corporation, the large mortgage insurer, also vetted and blessed the ITIN mortgage product. Just as there is no law in the United States that curtails property ownership by foreign nationals, so there are no boundaries to home ownership.

The same banks were balking at opening accounts for immigrants—and others, as we have seen—therefore complicating and extending the dimensions of the "unbanked" because of the problems stemming from the passage of the Patriot Act in the wake of 9/11. In many ways it is unclear why the solution was not as seamless as the use of ITINs, if the banks had really had their hearts in the business. Section 326 of the Patriot Act requires that a financial institution has to "verify identity of the customer" and the Secretary of the Treasury was to determine a system for attaining tax identification for foreign nationals, but all that means is an ITIN. This may have been a case where federal banking lobbyists were simply looking after the big guys and not the little ones, and could not keep their eyes on the prize in the push for post-9/11 legislation and joined with their conservative legal departments to hunker down in the hysteria after the attacks. Either way, as a University of Oregon report noted aptly, "The unintended effect was to deal a big blow to many community-based banks whose customers include a large number of undocumented immigrants."[24]

3

Stopping Foreclosures and Predatory Lending

In the last decade of the 20th century and the first decade of the 21st, there seemed to be significant progress in home ownership, especially among minority and lower-income households. But in the blink of an eye, most of the gains for minorities in home ownership over the last twenty years have been wiped out by the crises in the subprime lending sector.[1] Current estimates that another 5 million to 10 million homeowners are in danger of foreclosure underscore the dimensions of this crisis in home ownership.

Bizarrely, some of the rhetoric of the 2008 presidential campaign tried to target the Community Reinvestment Act (and even ACORN!) as culprits for the meltdown in housing and the excesses of subprime mortgage lending and securitization. This is a classic case of understanding the facts or, as Richard Pryor used to joke, your lying eyes. The problems in the subprime market could have been prevented, but the unwillingness to move quickly and move outside of the herd, driven by pursuit of what any casual reader of the daily papers knows now were false profits, was the undoing of the housing industry and triggered the collapse of the economy.

What in the world happened here? This is a story with several twists and turns, and surprisingly I found myself, as Chief Organizer of ACORN, sitting right across the table from many of these companies as they were caught like deer in the headlights of hubris and greed.

The Subprime Housing Market

At the core of this tragedy are different kinds of business models directed at increasing citizen wealth. The creation of a subprime housing market, for example, was supposed to be a boon to lower-income families seeking to be homeowners. In practice, too many of the subprime lenders and their practices turned into predators, ultimately devastating millions of home-seeking families. The subprime housing market was in turn caught up in the collapse of the housing bubble, destroying a number of the enabling financial institutions and the empires built on them.

In discussions with company after company from New Century to Option One to Countrywide, one set piece of my rap was that ACORN members believed in an active and vital subprime housing market, because many of our members could potentially benefit from a well-run mortgage market of this kind. This is because many of our lower-income and working families had experienced credit challenges and other economic problems that would normally shut them out of home ownership if they did not have recourse to a subprime market. The executives I talked to would often nod knowingly and, almost reading from their own script, talk about how much they believed in their business model as a "service to the community" and welcomed the discussions. Initially, in late 2006 and early 2007, these discussions were "baby and bathwater" conversations. The baby we wanted to keep alive and well was in fact the subprime mortgage market, while the bathwater that had to go was the array of predatory practices that had sprung up throughout these markets.

Financial Justice Campaigns

Well before the explosion of subprime lending, ACORN financial justice campaigns had targeted what we believed were the predatory practices of three companies: Ameriquest, Household Finance, and Wells Fargo. Our strategy had been numbingly straightforward. We would go after the largest subprime lender, and then number 2, then 3, and so on. Ameriquest became one of the centerpiece actions at ACORN's 2002 National Convention in Philadelphia. The company had an operation in the Philadelphia suburbs in what for the life of me looked like horse country. Thirty or more miles outside of Center City, we rode around looking for the home of one of their chief executives, in what finally turned out to be a fantabulous McMansion. We also burst into an office complex downtown where Ameriquest had its offices, to the surprise and somehow to the appreciation of Adam Bass, the senior vice president and general counsel at the time, and someone very well connected as the son-in-law to the majordomo of the company, Roland Arnall, a relationship that ended up being pivotal to this campaign.

Ameriquest seemed to have sprung from nowhere in Orange County, California, to become a leading mortgage lender, writing more mortgages than almost any other institution in the country. Unfortunately, we kept hearing one complaint after another from our members and from other people who came through the housing counseling offices run by the ACORN Housing Corporation. The heart of the problem centered on Ameriquest's mortgage broker distribution network and its outsourcing of the actual lending. This problem of outsourcing lending was epidemic throughout the subprime sector. For all the complaints, claims, and settlements, none of these companies, whether their intentions were honorable or not, ever did a good job of supervising their broker networks, thereby allowing them to be fertile fields for consumer abuse and deception.

Bass was smart and shrewd. He had seen the number of ACORN members in Philadelphia, and he agreed immediately to negotiations to try to resolve the issues. He got the big picture, so he moved quickly to resolve the headache and came to an agreement on a set of best practices that would eliminate predatory conditions in Ameriquest's operations. Importantly, Ameriquest also agreed to reduce its dependence on the broker network and to use its own people, whom it would hire, train, and supervise, to ensure fairer, more transparent lending operations. A ten-city trial program was initiated as part of the agreement with a small amount of multiyear support to implement the program. Ameriquest benefited by being an early responder in this campaign, quickly realizing that it was smarter—and much cheaper—to settle and deal with the problems rather than endure a protracted war in public, in the courts, and in the marketplace. Other lenders had to learn that lesson the hard way, particularly Household Finance.

Predatory practices that robbed citizens of their home-based wealth were not difficult to spot. A 2002 handout by Arizona Attorney General Terry Godard's office does a good job of making the list of "warning signs" for consumers to identify predators:

1. High interest rates (way above those of prime lenders).
2. Excessive points, late charges, and prepayment penalties (the latter often blocking the ability to refinance out of a predatory loan without a huge transaction cost).
3. Credit insurance packing (an addition of useless and discretionary products).
4. Asset-based lending (a pernicious practice that is based on stripping out the equity with a loan that is not based on ability of the consumer to pay).
5. Misrepresentations (essentially a bait-and-switch at closing).
6. Loan flipping or multiple refinancing (pushing borrowers into a refinancing cycle with rising rates and closing costs past affordability).
7. Balloon payments (with a large "death sentence" payment due at the end of the loan).
8. High closing costs (wrapping fees into the loan, forcing interest payments to be made on them).
9. Deceptive loan servicing (unsatisfactory loan statements that leave payments and accounts a guessing game).
10. Home improvement loans.
11. Loan broker fees (a siphoning of commissions from the loan proceeds, often without borrower notice or understanding).
12. Signing over the deed (a gratuitous offer to protect the homeowner from foreclosure, but often intended to rob the owner of the house).
13. Stop-payment advice (recommendations to stop payments, jeopardizing the note and forcing foreclosure).
14. Discrimination (of the garden variety, charging of different rates to women, older adults, and minorities for loans).[2]

Predatory practices have run the range of the imagination as unscrupulous, often unlicensed and unsupervised brokers saw a pile of money in the form of citizen wealth gained through built-up equity and a weak will at the corporate or governmental level to protect citizens against the abuse.

The "best practices" agreements that ACORN negotiated would eliminate such abuses, increase disclosures and transparencies for the borrowers, enshrine the understandings in the operating and training manuals of the companies, provide hotlines for problems encountered by ACORN members, and mandate regular reviews of complaints and resolutions to enforce and implement the agreements. Sometimes, and this was the case with Ameriquest, signing any kind of an agreement with a company, including modifying predatory practices, was seen as controversial by other advocates or community coalitions. This is often the tension faced by a community organization that has to answer to a membership that wants solutions to its grievances in specific and broad terms and insists on accountability to such standards, as opposed to advocates and policy experts, who are able to define their positions in a different part of the world from lower-income families. Voltaire's warning about not allowing the "best to become the enemy of the good" comes to mind here.[3] There are merits in all of these positions, and they are strongly and determinedly held, but there are different actors involved with widely disparate constituencies that must be served. On the whole, though, the disagreements have been understandable as part of the process of protecting and increasing citizen wealth.

Chicago-based Household Finance (HFC) was a more determined target. The company was not an upstart in this business, but was a longtime player with a broader product line, including credit cards (even the Union Privilege card offered by the AFL-CIO to its member unions, which arguably funded most of the AFL's organizing program throughout the period of its agreement with Household).[4] Nonetheless, HFC specialized in subprime lending, and for all of the billions of dollars' worth of mortgages HFC facilitated there were predatory issues with way too many. HFC's attitude to the ACORN campaign was stand and fight, so this campaign was long and drawn out.

ACORN threw the kitchen sink at Household Finance. There were actions at lending offices all around the country. We collected cases of what seemed to us to be predatory practices and turned them over to consumer advocates and attorneys general all over the country. We did study after study to try to document that Household Finance was up to no good. Lisa Donner, the head of the ACORN Financial Justice Center at that time, cultivated contacts among Wall Street analysts and was constantly on the phone with them to make sure they understood the business practices of the company and the problems they might raise. HFC's chief executive, William Aldinger, stood his ground. Despite everything we did, we could not budge Household either through the front door or behind the scenes, so, in a classic last-ditch maneuver common to so many organizing campaigns, we went to court with a class action suit in various jurisdictions with lawyers we recruited into the fray: my old friend Sara Siskind from Miner Barnwell's office in Madison, Wisconsin, and Niall McCarthy from Burlingame, California, who had experience engaging Household legally in the sometimes friendly California court system. A group of attorneys general from a number of states subsequently filed suit, using many of the cases in their states that we had initiated.

Litigation is never a promising avenue for community groups in campaigns. It is a tactic of last resort because it moves the field of battle to a distant location that cannot easily be impacted by a group's membership, in venues so formal as to be totally foreign. All of which is another way of saying that it was difficult, no matter how closely involved I was in the campaign, to know exactly what led to a complete resolution and settlement in our favor. Several things no doubt were at play:

- Household was bought by the giant banking conglomerate HSBC, headquartered in the United Kingdom. Shortly after the purchase, HSBC sent word that it planned to retain William Aldinger as CEO, but that it saw ACORN as a potential partner and ally in the United States.
- The approval of the class-action status of the ACORN litigation against Household, which signaled fully that this matter was not going away.
- The parallel pressure of the push from the state attorneys general on a similar litigation strategy, that even though not coordinated with ACORN's, was compatible in goals and aims, putting increased pressure on Household to come to a settlement.
- The fact that increasingly the "best practices" reforming predatory practices by Household were becoming seen as inevitable and commonplace, and therefore not worth the opposition and the negative impact on the company.

But, as I said, who knows? The point instead is that the environment seemed more and more to favor a settlement. Knowing later what I did not know then, I also suspect that HSBC was increasingly a voice in this process and above all else understood that an agreement with ACORN was essential to protect its international brand.

However it came to happen, the agreement was favorable to ACORN. The settlement with ACORN was for $484 million, with most of the money going into a homebuyers assistance program (to be administered by ACORN Housing) to refinance predatory loans and to provide assistance in getting homeowners back into affordable purchase programs. Interestingly, HSBC became a big supporter of this program, and its advocacy outlasted the settlement relief period.

Importantly for ACORN the agreement included $2 million per year each year for three years to increase our outreach efforts for home ownership, financial literacy, and membership and community benefits. We arrived at the figure of $2 million per year to support ACORN's remediation through a very simple formula. At one point in the middle of the ACORN campaign, Household had paid $1 million to Wade Henderson's Civil Rights Leadership Council, seemingly to have the council "front" for HFC's so-called "good" record. It seemed only just to me that if they were going to pay $1 million to have someone stand in our way, they ought to pay at least double that amount every year for real work to be done, and so our lawyers and negotiators were able to deliver justice on many fronts. Over the years, the relationship between ACORN and HSBC has increasingly focused on creating citizen wealth and has developed to be tremendously important to both parties, proving perhaps once again that bonds forged in fire prove stronger than any others.

ACORN's efforts with Wells Fargo provide a more cautionary tale for community groups that might try to duplicate this work. Much as Ameriquest had been the centerpiece of the ACORN National Convention in Philadelphia in 2002, Wells Fargo was the main target of 1500 marching ACORN members in downtown Los Angeles during the ACORN National Convention in 2004. The demand made by ACORN President Maude Hurd on the sidewalk—in front of the Wells Fargo building, within sight of the newly opened Walt Disney Concert Hall designed by Frank Gehry—was not about negotiations. The demand was to stop its predatory practices and to meet ACORN in court, and she turned over to the highest Wells Fargo executive on the sidewalk a copy of a suit filed that same day challenging the bank's predatory practices, as we had done with the Household Finance campaign. The actions against Wells Fargo found us confronting a deeply ideological opponent, a CEO who simply drew a line in the sand; every report we received said that he was unwilling to negotiate with ACORN under any circumstances. When business practices are trumped by personal animus, no one wins, and despite a similar campaign against Wells Fargo, our campaign was failing to get traction or draw blood, or even a reaction from the company. Worse, despite the "Hail Mary pass" of filing another lawsuit, the legal environment for class actions even in California had dramatically changed, creating huge obstacles for our success.

The footprint of the Wells Fargo abuse was national, but the eventual settlement was limited to relief in the state of California only. Most of the best practices demanded by ACORN were conceded, but Wells did so unilaterally to deny ACORN the ability to expand on or even enjoy the victory. The best practices agreed to were decent, but they trickled out as part of the company's practices rather than being imprinted indelibly as part of an agreed and enforced reform. The final settlement negotiations were as contentious as the entire campaign had been, making it harder to believe that Wells Fargo would emerge from the experience a better company with a deeper commitment to citizen wealth, and we have found that impression to be the case in confronting more recent problems with foreclosure modifications to Wells' portfolio.

The explosive growth of the subprime market ushered in a level of lender predation that defied belief, meeting little if any pretense of regulation by any potential regulatory body. The levels of hubris and greed were astounding.

A meeting in early 2007 with New Century at the company's offices in Orange County along with Jordan Ash, the second director of the ACORN Financial Justice Center, Bruce Dorpalen of ACORN Housing, and a number of ACORN leaders from California, saw it all on display. We were meeting with the company's newly minted CEO, several of the board members, and its general counsel, Terry Theologides, who was quite an up-and-comer in the industry at that time. We were worried about two issues that we wanted New Century to take the opportunity to solve. The first centered on its reliance on brokers, a practice that we had seen burn borrowers time after time. The New Century team claimed that they had rooted out the bad apples, turning some into local law enforcement or state attorneys general for prosecution and so forth, but they still did not convince us they could really adequately supervise these brokers or hold them accountable. When Jordan Ash raised the issue of their people in Texas double-charging on prepayment penalties, there was a visible gulp in the room, and the new CEO committed to investigating that problem immediately.

More telling was the problem of "stated income" loans in the New Century portfolio, and this became for us the harbinger of the disastrous collapse that was coming. In the same way that ACORN members believed that we needed a viable subprime market, we also believed that there was real value in "stated income" loans for some parts of our membership—tipped hospitality workers, for example, or self-employed business people. These were people whose income could not be simply determined by a W-2 tax statement from their employer. We believed that an individualized analysis of family income sources could often allow them to qualify for a loan that more traditional formulas would not allow. Tax returns could be a valid proof of reported income, for example, for small-business people or individual consultants or other self-employed workers over a certain number of years, even if the numbers were not verifiable from specific employers. Frequently in such cases a prospective homeowner could increase the down payment to qualify or in other ways "prove" the income.

These loans are often called "liar's loans" now, but practically speaking the problem was less in the loan itself than the almost total lack of effective supervision of the broker networks that were originating the loans. If there was a liar, the odds were that the broker was doing the lying more often than the homeowner. In modest neighborhoods we were finding elderly people with fixed incomes who were shocked to find that loan approval included an income figure "stated" at several times their actual income, and these instances were far too prevalent to have been coincidental. Such loans are just unprosecuted cases of fraud. Banks and mortgage companies are paid interest, points, and fees to calculate and manage risk, and to control their agents or brokers and broker networks. Stated income loans were not the problem, but management breakdowns in systems and supervision and the blind pursuit of quick and easy false profits were.

Nonetheless, we confronted New Century's top team with our inability to understand how, as the largest single mortgage originator in the United States at that time, almost half their loans were stated income loans. That defied belief and common sense at the same time. They hardly blinked.

We then were treated to a story about the sophistication of the company's computer programs in determining the accuracy and probability of loan issuances and success. In fact, every subprime company we met with—and on that day in Orange County, which is action central for subprime lenders, with so many of their headquarters there that we met with New Century, Ameriquest, and Option One—claimed to have world-class, Silicon Valley–certified, best-in-class computer programs that could calibrate risk down to the smallest decimal point. These claims proved again the truth of the adage "garbage in, garbage out" when it comes to computer systems, since none of the programs in the end protected these lenders from billion-dollar losses and bankruptcies. Another story that I will never forget is listening to the new CEO, Brad Morrice, explain that he had "drunk his own Kool-Aid" by getting an option ARM (adjustable rate mortgage) on his own house. I wonder if he still has a roof over his head, since he certainly does not have a job there.

I could tell many stories of sitting across table after table trying—and often succeeding—to win best-practice loan modifications from a host of different lenders at the top of the industry from Wall Street to Main Street. ACORN teams met with Countywide, the largest of the lenders, and negotiated a best-practices standard in the industry in 2007 that was announced in early 2008 on the eve of its purchase by Bank of America. We met with Litton, EMC, and Ocwen (after a long, hard campaign and pressure on its VA contract); Merrill Lynch, which owned several loan servicers; Deutsche Bank and Credit Suisse, which were trustees for huge syndication pools of loans; Citibank; and HSBC, coming to agreement with many of them about how to stave off foreclosures. In most cases the relief was generalized across their portfolio of loans but provided special relief for ACORN members and ACORN cases in our communities, giving an important organizational advantage to the solutions.

In no case were these agreements easy, because the industry was pushing to get to the front of the line when it came to making the loans and collecting the interest payments and fees, but was at the back of the line in terms of courage and values when it came to protecting citizen wealth in home ownership. To me, that seems virtually a criminal paradox.

The Subprime Implosion and Foreclosures

The subprime implosion has had severe impacts all across the country. We can get a sense of the dimensions of the resulting wave of foreclosures and impacts on citizen wealth from a report on the Kansas City area by the Center for Responsible Lending (CRL), one of the best community resources in this area. In Clay County alone at the end of 2007, CRL found that 816 homes with 2005/2006 subprime mortgages had foreclosed. Another 27,000 had lost value because of these foreclosures, and the county tax base had declined by an estimated $32.9 million.[5]

This snapshot suggests a picture of what is going on around the U.S. In October 2007, the Kansas City area ranked 14th in the severity of the foreclosure crisis. CRL estimates in a January 2008 report that 40.6 million neighboring homes will lose value because of subprime foreclosures, that the total decline in house values and the tax base from foreclosures will be $202 billion, and that homeowners will lose an average of $5000 each just because they live near a foreclosed house.[6]

Foreclosures simply make no sense for the lender, the homeowner, or the community. Every institution concedes the high cost of foreclosures. Carrying costs for the lender range from $45,000 to $59,000 to maintain, protect, and dispose of the property.[7] Studies indicate that a foreclosed and abandoned house also impacts entire communities, and therefore all of the families—and lenders—in the community. These studies report that the value of housing falls by 1 percent to 2 percent within a half-mile of an abandoned and empty house in a community.[8]

Recent work by the Joint Economic Committee of Congress puts average foreclosure costs at $77,934, while the cost to prevent a foreclosure runs to $3300.[9] This research breaks the loss down in the following piles:

1. The loss to the homeowner is $7200—there goes the citizen wealth.
2. Neighbors in close proximity lose $1508 as the value of their own homes falls.
3. Local government loses $19,227 in taxes and fees on the shrinking tax base as home values plummet.
4. The lender loses about $50,000.[10]

If you cannot accept government figures here, then let us look at something more business friendly, like Standard & Poor's, which considers only the $50,000 lost by the lender. S&P estimates the cash loss on the property at $40,000 (for a typical loan size of $210,000), and pegs more than a quarter of the loan amount for the costs of foreclosure. Included as well are payment of property taxes, hazard insurance, legal fees, appraisal, lost revenue, marketing fees, and home maintenance in various amounts.[11]

It all adds up, but none of it adds up to make foreclosures a good proposition for either business or the community. Lenders and policy makers talk about "moral hazard," which seems to mean that someone should suck it up and take a beating, but the day business puts any kind of "moral" anything ahead of a solid business decision, there will be snow in New Orleans in July.

In essence, everyone loses collectively, and when foreclosures hit the epidemic proportions we are seeing today, an entire community begins to decline. That translates into the value of homes sliding down virtually across the country, pushing millions of families "under water," meaning their house is worth considerably less than they owe, and meaning as well a huge loss in the citizen wealth that comes from home equity.

The response from the industry, regulators, and government (legislative and executive) has been tepid and ineffective and notable mostly for the length of the press releases rather than the effectiveness of blocking foreclosures. Relief programs continue to be praised and passed, but most on the broadest scale continue to be modifications that provide no real relief in terms of interest rate reductions or reductions in the size of the debt.

Public Goals and Private Enterprise

This is the fundamental paradox of citizen wealth. The United States as a matter of public policy and frequent pronouncement clearly believes in the alleviation of poverty and especially in the process of asset building through home ownership. Yet governmental inactivity in the face of the rapaciousness of many of the subprime lenders and of the unrestrained and unscrupulous practices of brokers and agents on the front line of the mortgage origination and distribution system undermines at every turn the foundation principles of citizen wealth by allowing home equity to be stripped almost as soon as it is built. Any cases would be too many cases.

The root of the conflict can be found in contradictions between public goals and private enterprise.

A subprime lending system that allows working families access to mortgage funds is a good and fair thing. There should be public encouragement of any asset building system that lowers the barrier to families and lessens their dependency on preexisting wealth. Reducing requirements for down payments for many of these mortgage products was a good thing. Even allowing some level of higher interest rate to offset the additional risk of a borrower's credit history is defensible, because the huge benefits of building long-term citizen wealth justify accepting risk on both sides.

ARMs

The problems of adjustable rate mortgages and affordability, though, are central to the foreclosure crisis and less defensible. The fraudsters who misstated incomes and used bait-and-switch interest rates often blatantly ignored whether or not the loan was actually affordable by the family on a long-term basis independent of future refinancings premised on rising market values. To understand both the problems and the solutions, you have to ignore all the background noise and distractions and focus on one overriding issue: Would the family be able to afford to make the payments and stay in the house under the terms of the agreement for the life of the loan independent of everything else? If subprime loans had been made on that basis, there would have been no significant difficulties and families would have been able to access home ownership and avoid foreclosure, barring unforeseen circumstances like job losses or health catastrophes. Since we and others were unable to convince companies to embrace the standard of affordability of loans as the bedrock under which all loans were made, an unsustainable real estate disaster was created that victimized the borrowers and eventually the entire economy.

Adjustable rate mortgages, or ARMs as they are more popularly known, in theory allowed a homeowner to enter the loan at a lower interest rate with an adjustable increase in the rate in two or three years, allowing borrowers to believe that one of two things might work for them: Either their incomes might have increased so that they would have a higher credit rating and could afford the jump, or value of the property would have increased and they would then be able to refinance into a better rate for a longer-term fixed mortgage. This model falls apart when recession sets in, jobs are lost, and housing prices do not inexorably increase, leaving millions of homeowners needing a break that isn't going to come. It is hard to believe that the banking industry did not fully appreciate the risk of using what they called "teaser" rates that masked an inability of many families to sustain the loan. In such a bait-and-switch environment it is amazing that even in worst cases on 2/28s and 3/27s the default rate has not surpassed 10 percent for most companies.

When we survey neighborhood residents few people seem to understand that they have ARMs—despite the mountains of paper required for disclosures by the government at closing. This was a new and sophisticated product and the lack of supervision of the broker networks by many of the companies meant that the Wild West could prevail at the grassroots level. Many prospective borrowers were unaware of the time bomb ticking in their loans until they found that they were unable to make the mounting payments, often discovering too late that their incomes had been exaggerated by their mortgage brokers.

Option ARMs were one of the most outrageous examples of super-sophisticated products that were foisted on working families. These loans carried adjustable interest rates, but here ordinary homeowners would be playing their own type of arbitrage every month on whether to make a payment at all or simply pay some of the interest or pay just about whatever they felt like paying. There is a story I heard so often during our negotiations with Countrywide that repetition alone ought to have made it real rather than apocryphal. Countrywide sold a lot of option ARMs, and we believed that the company widely marketed the product in lower-income and minority communities, especially in California. Countrywide's founder and CEO, Angelo Mozilo, believed that borrowers would make sophisticated decisions about payments and tend to make monthly payments on principle rather than allowing the size of the loan to balloon by making minimal to no payments. He supposedly asked for and got a random list of a couple of dozen of such option ARM loans and personally called the borrowers to ask how they were handling the payments. He quickly found to his dismay that no one was making any more than interest payments to keep the loan current. He as quickly realized that he needed to sell his baby, Countrywide, while there was still something to sell rather than watch the company sink to nothing, as Ameriquest did before being bought by Citibank, or relive the failure to sell Option One that had caught the head of H&R Block.

The simplest test of the loans that could have achieved policy and public goals while preventing the meltdown of the housing market and wiped out billions of dollars in citizen wealth would have been to require affordability as the criterion for making loans. An affordability standard would have been based not simply on the two- or three-year period covered by the teaser rate, but on the ability of the family to make the payments within reasonable income expectations for the remaining life of the loan.

The securitization of so many of these loans by nonbank institutions that were not required to portfolio the loans on their own balance sheets contributed to the lack of transparency, the failure to properly assess risk, and the deer-in-the-headlights lack of leadership by financial institutions of all shapes and sizes. In this "brave new world" of postmodern lending we found little bravery. Larry Litton of Litton Loan Servicing in Houston was perhaps the exception proving the rule. He was one of the earliest voices arguing at the outset of the crisis in the loudest possible terms that all borrowers his firm was handling should simply get an automatic two-year freeze at the introductory or teaser rate. When he made that offer to an ACORN delegation meeting with him at his home office that included me, Toni McElroy, and Leonard Smith, we should have stopped that minute, gotten him to sign on the dotted line, and quickly pushed the rest of the industry to adopt that minimum standard. As it was, we got caught up in negotiations with company after company while the crisis deepened and modifications were slow in coming while companies waited for others or for the government to step in and more families lost their houses.

Coming to a first-of-its-kind agreement with Countrywide made a huge difference in achieving improved agreements with HSBC and Citibank, among others, but many of these companies lacked the courage to publicly announce their new practices, even when some of them were superior to those in the agreement Countrywide had signed. Part of the problem was the market, but the rest of the problem they claimed was fear of litigation, though lawyers have really been the least of the problems in the subprime implosion. The real leverage the companies were exercising was the Treasury Department, the Federal Reserve, and the federal government itself, and that is where they ran, no matter how slowly, in packs as every announcement did little but give them cover. The banks and loan servicers would comment frankly on the ineffectuality of the announcements and proposals as little more than press puffery, but they would sign on nonetheless to cover themselves.

Credit Desert

The disturbing problem for the future for lower-income families trying to access the assets of home ownership is whether the credit crisis becomes institutionalized as a new version of systemic redlining of neighborhoods. There is no subprime lending market now whatsoever. Loans in lower-income communities are now being done only at the credit standards set by Fannie Mae and Freddie Mac so that institutions can offload them to the secondary market. In terms of credit scores, that often means a 650 FICA score or higher where previously a working family could aspire to home ownership with a credit score of as low as 500 to 550 with good credit counseling.

A credit desert in lower-income communities where only the best credit history and scores can qualify a family for home ownership does not return us to the worst days of before CRA, but raises the specter of huge credit shortages in lower-income communities and the twin problem of declining opportunities to build citizen wealth. There are still many institutions that would prefer not to lend in such neighborhoods if they perceive the slightest risk, and proving discrimination under the new credit conditions and a diluted legal regime will be daunting. This is a problem without a plan.

Paradoxically, the federal bailout of Fannie Mae and Freddie Mac should herald quite a different response. These quasi-federal/quasi-private corporations are now being propped up by the full resources and credit of the United States government. It would seem high time to stop the charade that these are private enterprises, paying hundreds of executives million-dollar-plus salaries, and turn the clock back sixty years to the time when they were created to allow a secondary market to help families hold on to and acquire homes after the Great Depression. Whether by hook or crook, lower-income families are now back in the same depths of a citizen wealth depression when it comes to acquiring homes in the 21st century, and we should completely federalize these two entities in order to achieve the goals of providing home ownership opportunities to low- and moderate-income families.

If not, then the path to citizen wealth for such families will be immeasurably steeper, through no fault of these families, but to their permanent peril.

4

Making Work Pay Living Wages

There is nothing that confronts American mythology more directly than the reality of men and women and their families working at their jobs, and working hard, but still not achieving economic security simply because they are not making a living wage. In the modern economy, dominated by service rather than manufacturing jobs and increasing skill and educational requirements, making work pay more is the only real strategy for increasing incomes and thus citizen wealth.

The best alternative to a lower-wage job is no longer to think of such jobs as "starter" jobs, temporary jobs, extra jobs, or part-time jobs. Most employees who hold these positions change jobs constantly in the service economy, which dominates employment in the 21st-century economy. They're searching for the greener grass at the next store down the mall, but most people never find it. Simply stated, then, it might be best to figure out a way to raise the wages where you are rather than either to grin and bear it or to job-hop from place to place.

There is no need to quibble over an exact number that defines a "living wage" or "family-supporting wage" or whatever someone might want to call it. We have spent too much time on that argument, and lost too many campaigns having fallen in love with a number rather than having worked the political equation through to an effective solution. The numbers are easily available, though, and they range from

$10 to $15 per hour, depending on where the family lives and works and what is included or excluded. Here it is enough to say that such a wage is many dollars more than the minimum or average wages most workers receive. The point is that there are things that can be done and have been proven to push wages closer to making work pay, and we all need to do a lot more of this on a continual basis.

Once again, community organizations and community/labor–based coalitions have led the way in devising some important and effective strategies for meeting the issues of income and jobs head on. These campaigns to help working families take longer strides toward citizen wealth have been difficult, and hard lessons have been learned about victories being more incremental than comprehensive, more broad based than narrowly defined. But importantly, they have proven time and time again that hard work can be rewarded and that progress can be won by citizens working together to increase incomes and therefore build the preconditions for citizen wealth.

The Living Wage Movement

Most of us date the beginning of what has come to be called the living wage movement to an effort undertaken in late 1994 by BUILD, a community organization associated with the Industrial Areas Foundation (founded by the renowned organizer Saul Alinsky). BUILD pushed for and won a novel program in Baltimore that provided higher wages for municipally contracted services. An earlier effort had been undertaken successfully by the Calumet Project for Industrial Jobs in Gary, Indiana, in January 1991 to provide prevailing wages and full healthcare, which was also a community-based effort that worked on labor issues and community organizing. The City of Des Moines, Iowa, had on its own initiated a base pay rate of $7 an hour even earlier, in 1988, for city-funded projects.[1]

When ACORN embarked on its living wage campaign in many of the cities and states where we were organizing, we had no idea at the time that this history was so rich. Our analysis was simpler and perhaps more desperate. As an organization of lower- and moderate-income families, we had been committed for many years to gaining increases in the federal minimum wage. Our hopes had originally been high for such an increase with the advent of the Clinton administration, since there had rarely been a Democratic administration that had not raised

the federal minimum wage. We were even more optimistic when Labor Secretary Robert Reich publicly endorsed a program of indexing
the federal minimum wage to inflation or the consumer price index,[2]
which would mean that the long dry periods between official increases
would finally be ended and the wage would more adequately reflect a
figure corresponding to the basic needs for workers and their families.
When the Fair Labor Standards Act had originally been passed in 1938,
part of the idea behind the measure was to cover the costs of food,
clothing, and shelter. In the last seventy years, the purchasing power
of the minimum wage has steadily lost ground to inflation because
of infrequent updates and is now unmoored to anything other than
political will—something that has often been lacking.

I had gotten the bad news directly from Tom Glynn, the deputy secretary of the Department of Labor (DOL), over lunch in the department cafeteria, only moments after he had introduced me to Secretary
Reich as he jumped on a special elevator. Tom was an old friend from
back in the day, when we both worked in Boston with the Massachusetts Welfare Rights Organization in the late 1960s, where he had been
an assigned VISTA and then a full-time staffer. The news was discon-
certing. The White House had issued an order that anything to do
with the minimum wage (and a lot of other programs), and especially
indexing, was to be put on the back burner so that the administration
could focus on trying to pass comprehensive healthcare reform. From
that meeting on, the writing was on the wall. If we were going to
deliver wage increases to our low-wage members, we were going to
have to find another way to do so, because we were not going to see
a federally mandated increase.[3]

As we discussed this situation afterward among ACORN staff and
leaders, we remembered the strategies that we had employed to try
to offset the wave of inflationary rate increases in gas and electric
utilities in the 1970s that had hammered our members so badly in
Arkansas and other states. We had gone to the ballot locally in Little
Rock and other Arkansas cities, as well as statewide in Missouri and
South Dakota, to try to win "lifeline" utility rates that would provide
a flat-rate ("necessity") level for the first 400 kilowatts of electricity
usage. We pushed this issue so that lower-income and senior citizens
would have a buffer against the spiking utility rates and shutoffs. We
decided to go back to that well and look state by state and city by city

to see where we could legally bring initiatives that would increase the minimum wage across entire governmental jurisdictions.

Our first living wage targets were Denver and Houston in the late 1990s,[4] and we were ambitious. These were citywide initiatives that would raise wages for all workers across the board within these municipalities. We were asking for at least $6.50 per hour in both communities.[5] Since these were our first efforts, we tried to peg the wages at the middle to the top end of what we thought *real* living wages might be in these communities. In Houston, where our initiative made the ballot as part of a coalition driven by Local 100 of the Service Employees International Union (SEIU) and ACORN, this wage would have represented a raise of almost 20 percent above the federal minimum wage of $5.15. In Denver the level was about the same. The petitioning in Houston was linked to the City Council elections in November.[6] Orell Fitzsimmons from Local 100 had directed the campaign, and the early polls were very encouraging. Local 100 members in the Houston Independent School District stood to benefit hugely, since they were stuck in lower-wage occupations in the food service, custodial, and transportation departments. They worked unstintingly in the campaign, as did many ACORN members. Andy Stern, the newly elected international president of SEIU, delivered on his commitment to play a more activist role in the South and came to Houston to help publicize the campaign and get out the vote in the week before the election, visiting some of the school cafeterias, doing radio spots, and meeting with backers such as Congresswoman Sheila Jackson Lee.

What we did not predict was the money poured into the campaign by the opposition during the closing two weeks of the campaign from the Hotel and Restaurant Association, and the big hitters for the association were none other than McDonald's, Burger King, and other fast-food chains. The TV ads were subtle but powerful, and pushed the theme that essentially we were trying to do the right thing, but that our method was wrong and that people would lose jobs if our initiative won.

On election night we found that we had lost badly overall, but we had rocked in our wards. We had won the 3rd and 5th Wards where the bulk of lower-income and working families lived, especially Latinos and African Americans. We did well in the precincts where we had support, but we were beaten like a drum across the rest of the city by about a three-to-one margin, with our team on the "one" side. We got only one vote in the Houston River Oaks precinct where former President George H. W. Bush lived. I used to joke with my *compañero* Orell that they are *still looking* for the one vote we got in that neighborhood for a minimum wage increase!

Our Denver initiative was similar, calling for a minimum wage of $7.25 rather than $7.50. More than $1 million was put together by the same fast-food and hospitality-based companies, and the result was also the same—a three-to-one shellacking of ACORN's initiative. In both cases, we learned some hard lessons that helped us build our organizing skills, but we had been unsuccessful in advancing citizen wealth. Instead, we tacked in a different direction, making the size of the hourly increases more modest and less pronounced and playing "small ball" on contracts, a strategy that for a while seemed more promising.

Our pursuit of smaller-scale increases for lower-wage workers was essentially a "prevailing wage" strategy, similar to what is built in to federal law covering federal contracts for construction work (the Davis-Bacon Act), shipbuilding (the McCarran-Ferguson Act), and service work (the Service Contract Act). The strategy was to set a floor for minimum wages that could be paid for all contract work from a jurisdiction, either a city or a county. ACORN initiated successful efforts along these lines in Minneapolis, St. Paul, and Boston in the wake of the Denver and Houston defeats.

At the same time, SEIU Local 100, ACORN, United Teachers of New Orleans/AFT, and the Greater New Orleans AFL-CIO continued attempts to get a citywide increase of $1.00 over the federal minimum wage on the ballot as part of a strategy for effective but more modest increases that might find sufficient electoral support to pass. This strategy was based on the relatively noncontroversial measure enacted in the District of Columbia in 1992 that set an "automatic" minimum wage at $1.00 higher than the federal minimum. In New Orleans, this coalition sought to use the D.C. measure as a precedent for raising wages in a similar way.

In the ten-year period from 1996 to 2006 the ACORN Living Wage Center, based in Washington, D.C., was able to document more than 140 successful living wage efforts, the vast majority of which were contract-based, prevailing-wage campaigns. Some of these efforts had broad impacts, like the Boston and Chicago efforts led by ACORN in coalition with central labor bodies and individual unions, and the benchmark standard achieved by the Los Angeles Alliance for a New Economy (LAANE) headed by Madeline Janis-Aparicio. In each of these cases thousands of publicly contracted workers saw significant increases in their wages.

Other efforts have been criticized from both the left and right, and even by living wage advocates, for having achieved legislative victories but often impacting so few workers as to be inconsequential. Admittedly, some of these ordinances helped relatively few workers, but the ordinances often served as an effective buffer against contracting out public jobs with relatively high pay and benefits to private sector bidders that would have paid near the minimum wage with few if any benefits.

Living wage campaigns also created tremendously effective alliances between community groups and organized labor around issues of citizen wealth—and it would be a mistake to believe that these alliances were either easy or natural for either party. In fact, at the start of many of the living wage campaigns, even unions that we thought would be automatic allies sometimes worried that joining in a public fight for a higher wage would seem to reflect negatively on their power at the bargaining table. I can vividly remember the long hours that ACORN organizer Derecka Mehrens spent convincing the president of a Hotel Workers local in San Jose. He was afraid his members would feel that the union was weak if it supported a wage floor outside the collective bargaining agreement. All of these efforts required some rethinking about roles, tactics, and strategies more attuned to a modern-day reevaluation of the relative strengths and weaknesses of labor unions versus community-based initiatives. On the living wage front, labor unions many times played a stronger role behind the scenes, so their support would not seem too self-interested.

Unions like SEIU Local 100,[7] which was active in these efforts in the middle South states of Arkansas, Louisiana, and Texas, looked at these issues from a different strategic perspective. The prevailing wage standard protected work and set a benchmark. If it was possible to achieve a citywide standard for all work, then a new baseline level for wages would be set, in turn raising all boats by setting a new minimum standard, and thereby allowing collectively bargained wages to rise along with these minimums. Additionally, in Local 100's case virtually all of its contracts with both public and private sector workers contained re-opener clauses calling for renegotiation if there was a local, state, or federal minimum wage increase; others called for an automatic increase that protected the contract wages from compression with the new minimum wage. For Local 100's lower-wage service sector members a living wage campaign was a case of "heads we win, tails we win." Not every union had such contract language, and other unions enjoyed wage levels so far above the minimum wage that the ripple impact of such increases would be negligible for them, but that was certainly not the case for the newly organized southern service sector and hospitality workers.

Local 100 SEIU was certainly not unique. Many unions also found that their active and enthusiastic participation in living wage coalitions directly benefited their members. Certainly, the Hotel Employees and Restaurant Employees (HERE), SEIU, United Food and Commercial Workers (UFCW), and others all benefited from the leverage that grew out of living wage efforts in Los Angeles. Amy Dean, the former president of the Central Labor Council in San Jose, and leader of the Union Cities program under the AFL-CIO in that capacity, has frequently noted how important community/labor coalitions were in advancing the ability of labor to achieve its objectives and working partnerships in this key central labor council during the 1990s.[8] SEIU 880 in Chicago, representing home healthcare workers, has frequently argued that the ability to raise wages because of the Chicago living wage ordinance helped them leverage the rates for thousands of workers they represented at the state level. Application of the living wage ordinances in Los Angeles and San Francisco leveraged the organization of thousands of airport workers as these measures were extended to cover such public authorities as well.

Business and industry clearly understood the power of areawide campaigns to increase the minimum wage. Extensive efforts were made by restaurant associations, hotel associations, and independent small business groups to lobby legislatures to amend state laws to prevent cities from passing such increases. Their efforts were initially concentrated in states like Colorado and Texas where we had already had some success and commercial interests wanted to lock the door to the future. After bitter fights in both states, cities lost the ability to regulate matters affecting such wage increases through the initiative process. Similar efforts were undertaken in Louisiana, Florida, and other southern states with various levels of success to limit the ability of local jurisdictions to raise wages.

Although the effort to put a $1.00 increase in the minimum wage on the ballot in New Orleans through the initiative process had been blocked temporarily by legal maneuvers, the local courts finally allowed it to proceed to election. The opposition, led by the Louisiana Restaurant Association and the local hotel association, sought to raise $500,000 to $1,000,000 for the campaign with constant exhortations through their website and bulletins, but their core strategy seemed to be legal delays and obfuscation. Once the election was inevitable, however, they seemed to concede that the poverty of the city and its general demographics favored the living wage coalition, along with the fact that we were "allowing people to vote themselves a raise." After a bitterly fought campaign New Orleans voters approved its first-ever citywide minimum wage increase by a healthy margin of 63 percent to 37 percent in February 2002. Tipped employees were covered, an important provision in an economy dominated by jobs in the hospitality sector, with the only exemptions being for smaller businesses (those with less than $500,000 in annual revenue) and public employees. Predictably, the opposition went to court almost immediately to block implementation of the measure. The early court decisions favored ACORN, SEIU Local 100, and its allies when local judges refused to block implementation. The issue in contention was an end-run by industry to the conservative Louisiana legislature to repeal a city's ability to regulate local wages *after* the New Orleans measure had been filed for the ballot. The Appeals Court, in one of the last decisions made by former New Orleans Mayor and HUD Secretary Maurice "Moon" Landrieu, ruled in favor of the living wage advocates. The Louisiana Supreme Court accepted the case and finally yielded to the pressure, despite excellent arguments by the coalition's lawyers Louis Robein, the premier labor lawyer in the city, and Bill Quigley, one of the most activist civil rights lawyers in New Orleans, voiding the measure late in 2002.

New Mexico was another battleground. Similar efforts to increase minimum wages even more substantially were heading toward the ballot around this same time in Albuquerque and Santa Fe. ACORN largely led the coalition in Albuquerque but failed in its early attempts to win a place on the ballot, while a living wage coalition in Santa Fe made great progress in that city and was successful. The measure in Santa Fe had real weight. The provisions would create a citywide living wage of $8.50 for any establishment employing over twenty-five workers. There would also be a bump every two years of an additional dollar until $10.50 per hour would be reached in 2008, and from that point forward the rate would be indexed to inflation. An election was avoided in Santa Fe when the City Council approved the increase over the shouts and protests of opponents. Legislative end-runs had been blocked in New Mexico despite earlier efforts, and the court challenges were in the end unsuccessful, so a citywide living wage campaign finally emerged with a victory.

The Santa Fe victory in February 2003 was followed later in the year by an equally important win in San Francisco in November 2003, when voters there approved an $8.50 citywide minimum wage after extensive work by a coalition led by Hotel Employees and Restaurant Employees Local 2 and its president, Mike Casey, along with San Francisco ACORN. The measure covered all businesses with ten or more employees and established annual indexing as well. California, as the most populous state in the country, continues to be a fertile field for advances in living wage provisions if community groups and labor, following the example of San Francisco's leaders, are able to put together the capacity and resources to provide, city by city, the leadership in advancing minimum wages.

Another important adaptation of the living wage strategy has more recently been attempts to increase the wages of retail workers. A coalition of community groups led by the UFCW and Chicago ACORN were concerned about Wal-Mart's efforts to build supercenters inside Chicago's city limits and attempted to apply the living wage standards to create a separate standard for retail workers. The Chicago City Council passed the measure but was not able to overturn the first veto in the administration of longtime Mayor Richard J. Daley. A recent effort led by WARN (the Wal-Mart Alliance for Reform Now) culminated in November 2007. It used a loophole in the repeal of a city's home rule rights to set wages in Florida that allowed an exception in the case of wages for any firms benefiting from subsidized employment. In Sarasota, along Florida's Gulf Coast, a Wal-Mart superstore had been proposed for an urban brownfield area in a largely African American community, but the project was conditioned on the city alleviating any environmental problems with the site. WARN and its allies were able to bring forward a petition setting a minimum wage for such subsidized projects with more than fifty employees; this rate would be double the minimum wage. The measure passed easily and went into effect without legal challenge as a first success of its kind nationally.

As powerful and effective as citywide measures have been in moving the living wage agenda forward, nothing has had such a dramatic impact as statewide minimum wage increases. Once again there were hard bumps in the road before community groups found the formula for success, but when it came the results were powerful. ACORN led a first effort in Missouri in 1996, with the campaign having been a major theme of the ACORN Convention in St. Louis held in that year. The threshold for initiative referendums at the state level was of course significantly greater and required huge resources and organizational capacity. For grassroots membership organizations of lower-income families the effort to qualify an initiative for the ballot was of such a magnitude and intensity that it exhausted the entire organization and its membership in the mere effort to qualify, leaving little left for the actual campaign to get out the vote and win the election. The first effort in Missouri, like those in Houston and Denver, taught us a lot of lessons but failed to secure a victory.[9]

ACORN made Florida the test case for this strategy in 2004 in a Herculean effort requiring almost 1 million signatures to qualify for the ballot in one of the largest states in the country and a huge battleground for that fall's presidential election. We made it onto the ballot, but that achievement was a miracle and required an effort so massive that it almost destroyed the basic organizational apparatus and set back other membership programs and activities. But it would be next to impossible to unravel that effort once we succeeded in securing a place on the ballot. In Florida, based on important lessons from the earlier campaigns, we had resisted temptations to pad the numbers higher and had stuck with the automatic dollar increase above the federal minimum wage, a position that was almost unassailable. Our voters, low- and moderate-income families seeking citizen wealth, had trouble believing that a $1.00 increase could really wreck the economy, which is what our opponents constantly tried to claim. Prior to the 2004 election a number of Florida communities had been devastated by not one but three hurricanes. The most frightening ad against our measure threatened a fourth wave of destruction after showing film footage of the hurricanes, with that wave being the minimum wage increase. In November, we won handily with 70 percent of the vote.

The impact of victory was so massive that despite the difficulty of its achievement it was hard to walk away from the intoxication of the results. The estimates from Robert Pollin and his associates were that 300,000 people would benefit directly from the increase and another 550,000 would receive wage increases because of the ripple impact,[10] because employers would try to maintain some margin between the new minimum wage and wages just above that level. This victory would thus yield $121.9 million in wage increases per year. In addition, it was a "gift that keeps on giving" in the sense that with every increase in the federal minimum wage the 2004 election results would be felt once again in the pocketbooks of lower-wage workers throughout Florida.

ACORN doubled down for the 2006 election, targeting a number of states, especially Missouri, Colorado, Ohio, and Arizona. We also worked with coalitions in other states to win additional increases in Michigan and Arkansas, among other places. Zach Polett, ACORN's political director, made the astute observation deep into the 2006 electoral cycle that, given the results, the largest error we made was in "not targeting *even more* states." He made this point after seeing legislators buckle in Michigan and Arkansas and preemptively increase state minimum wages to new highs rather than force community and labor coalitions to go the expensive and time-consuming route through initiative petitions and general election ballots. The efforts in these two states were more than feints, since signature efforts were already under way and resulted in increases from $5.15 to $7.40 in Michigan and from $5.15 to $6.25 in Arkansas. The opportunity to win higher increases and inflation indexing might have been lost in such compromises, but proponents of citizen wealth could hardly walk away with victories in hand without the expense of the contests. Polett's point was simple: We should have added another set of states and seen how many could have been pushed to adopt higher minimum wages with similar strategies.

In the big four states we targeted from the very beginning there was no way to win but straight up the middle, which meant millions of petition signatures and holding on to win in the 2006 mid-term elections in November. Once again, despite difficult campaigns victories were won in each state by solid margins:

Table 1 Votes on Minimum Wage Propositions

State	Votes For	Votes Against	Percentage For	Percentage Against
Ohio	2,080,648	1,622,772	56%	44%
Colorado	725,700	646,935	53%	47%
Arizona	756,144	393,393	66%	34%
Missouri	1,583,340	501,657	76%	24%

Source: "America Votes 2006," www.cnn.com/ELECTION/2006/pages/results/ballot.measures/.

And once again the magnitude of the victory was amazing when one looked at the impact on low-wage workers.

If we throw in the impact of the states listed in Table 2, then there is even more icing on the cake. Altogether, the transfer of income from employers to workers in these eleven states would conservatively add up to $16 billion. For ACORN and its allies, this made the entire effort worthwhile. Our cost was a direct expenditure of $4 million,[11] and indirect expenditures of perhaps another $4 million,[12] which included the value of the time ACORN members donated and time lost from other organizational activities. Amazingly, then, ACORN's investment of $8 million leveraged annual increases in income for 2007 of about $7 billion, which over five years would be $35 billion and ten years would reach $70 billion, and so on. It is hard to imagine a greater victory in terms of income transfers to lower-income and lower-waged families than was delivered by these minimum wage election victories in 2006.

Campaign Lessons

The efforts to build a movement to win living wages driven by community groups over the decade arguably increased the power of community organizations to an unparalleled level, but it also created a

Table 2 Results of Four State Minimum Wage Campaigns

	Ohio	Arizona	Missouri	Colorado
Minimum wage before increase	$5.15	$5.15	$5.15	$5.15
Minimum wage after increase	$7.25	$6.95	$6.50	$7.02
Number of workers directly affected	320,000	106,000	120,000	138,000
Number of workers indirectly affected	126,000	197,000	136,000	155,953
Total number of workers affected	446,000	303,000	256,000	293,953
Percent full time	75	60	51	51
Percent part time	25	40	49	49
Full-time increase in annual income	$4,368	$3,744	$2,808	$3,890
Part-time increase in annual income	$2,730	$2,340	$1,755	$2,431
Total full-time increase in annual income	$1.048 Billion	$238.1 Million	$171.8 Million	$273.8 Million
Total part-time increase in annual income	$218.4 Million	$99.2 Million	$103.2 Million	$164.4 Million
Amount gained by indirectly affected workers	$65.5 Million	$102.4 Million	$70.7 Million	$81.1 Million
Total amount gained	$1.332 Billion	$879.5 Million	$345.7 Million	$519.2 Million

political landscape around questions of income and citizen wealth that has helped change the outlook for the future. No matter how many times our opponents cried that the sky would fall if these small incremental wage increases were passed, the American public went to the polls and decisively voted to make work pay and to restore a basic justice and equity to the pay packages of lower-wage workers. By learning not to overreach ourselves but to peg the increases more modestly, we had hit a sweet spot that the voters appreciated and that business opposition could not destroy. Hope for higher wages began to trump the fear of lost jobs for America's lower-wage workers.

Table 3 Results of 2006 Minimum Wage Campaigns

	Illinois	Massachusetts	New Mexico	California
Minimum wage before increase	$6.50	$6.75	$5.15	$5.75
Minimum wage after increase	$7.75	$8.00	$7.50	$8.00
Number of workers directly affected	144,000	107,000	129,859	1,400,000
Number of workers indirectly affected	506,000	208,000	95,842	700,000
Total number of workers affected	650,000	315,000	225,701	2,100,000
Percent full time	70	46	51	63
Percent part time	30	54	49	37
Increase in income for full-time workers	$4,680	$4,680	$4,888	$4,680
Increase in income for part-time workers	$1,625	$1,625	$3,055	$2,925
Amount of increase for full-time workers	$471.7 Million	$230.3 Million	$323.7 Million	$4.128 Billion
Amount of increase for part-time workers	$70.2 Million	$93.9 Million	$194.4 Million	$1.515 Billion
Amount gained by indi-rectly affected workers	$263.1 Million	$108.2 Million	$49.8 Million	$364 Million
Total increase in annual wages	$2600	$2600	$4888	$4680
Total income gained	$1.610 Billion	$864.9 Million	$568 Million	$6.007 Billion

Table 3 Results of 2006 Minimum Wage Campaigns (Continued)

	Connecticut	Florida	Pennsylvania
Minimum wage before increase	$7.10	$5.15	$5.15
Minimum wage after increase	$7.65	$6.15	$7.15
Number of workers directly affected	39,000	304,000	510,000
Number of workers indirectly affected	42,000	464,000	350,000
Total number of workers affected	81,000	768,000	754,000
Percent full time	51	51	37
Percent part time	49	49	63
Increase in income for full-time workers	$1,144	$2,080	$4,680
Increase in income for part-time workers	$715	$1,300	$2,925
Amount of increase for full-time workers	$22.8 Million	$322.5 Million	$883.1 Million
Amount of increase for part-time workers	$13.7 Million	$193.6 Million	$939.8 Million
Amount gained by indirectly affected workers	$21.8 Million	$241.2 Million	$182.0 Million
Total increase in annual wages	$1,144	$2,080	$4,160
Total income gained	$58.3 Million	$2.272 Billion	$2.005 Billion

The other lesson often learned over the course of ACORN's history and discovered again so powerfully in these victories in city after city and state after state is that we had to be willing to take risks to win great victories, and the best risks to take were to try demonstrating *and* proving public support. Though winning was never certain and defeat could be debilitating, publicly proving support in significant numbers and voting strength built demonstrable power. If the purpose of community organizing is building power, these were referenda on the support and strength of community organizing converted into raw political capital that then became available for further advances.

The November 2006 elections saw control of Congress shift to the Democratic Party, which is ostensibly friendlier to increases in the federal minimum wage. After a long period during which the purchasing power of the minimum wage continued to fall, even President George W. Bush found it hard not to sign an increase to $5.85 an hour that became effective in July 2007, with another increase to $6.55 that was implemented in July 2008, and a final bump scheduled to move the minimum to $7.25 in July 2009. A new increase will be a political lift for a new president, but an alternative that might be politically more valuable and net a larger increase in citizen wealth would be to simply amend the existing act to index future increases for 2010 and beyond to the fixed hourly increase that has already been established. This might be politically a little easier for a new Congress and president and could allow other adjustments to normalize the rate once the critical indexing so important for low-wage workers is in place.

Congress could also see from the results of the 2006 elections that such increases were indisputably popular and there was a strong emerging constituency for equity and progress at the workplace. If the ideological battle to make work replace welfare had been won at the end of the 20th century, then the next battleground had to be proving that work could pay, or there would be no firm foundation supporting the myth of a new America where there is opportunity for all to build citizen wealth through work.

This may not have been how every member of Congress saw the issue when they passed the new federal minimum wage increase, but this was the way it really was and had to be.

5

Creating Wealth Through Worker Organizations

Andy Stern, president of the Service Employees International Union (SEIU), has repeatedly called unions "the nation's most effective poverty program."[1] Others have frequently credited union organization in the industrial sector in the middle years of the 20th century for creating a middle class in America. Yet without doubt it is also true that unions have become less and less able to deliver citizen wealth for rank-and-file workers.

If classically organized institutional unions cannot deliver more income because they are fighting for survival and are too weakened to do so, then we need alternative membership-based, worker-centered organizations working in concert with trade unions or independently to take up the slack. Such "majority unions" may look and feel different from the unions we are familiar with as part of the current collective bargaining environment. The almost unheralded but greatest organizing success among workers in the last forty years has in fact been among "informal" home health and home daycare workers. They have organized associations that have led to strong organizations and unions increasing wages, benefits, and economic security for more than half a million workers.

The labor movement at the beginning of the 21st century is a long way from delivering on either its historic record or its promise. Union membership density in the private sector has plummeted to the lowest figures in 100 years, with barely 8 percent of private sector workers now in unions.[2] Including the public sector with its higher level of union density, the overall level of union membership is 12.8 percent.[3] The last time American workers were so poorly represented by unions was 1902,[4] in the first decade of the 20th century.[5]

I happen to believe that unions are a great thing for workers, but even if I did not, and I believed that only citizen wealth was important, I would have to believe that labor being organized was an important achievement in realizing this objective because of the "union advantage," the differential in income enjoyed by workers who are unionized over workers who are not represented by unions. Most recently, this differential stood at $4 per hour.[6] Unionized manufacturing workers, who have enjoyed this advantage for a number of decades, have a $9-per-hour advantage over nonunion workers. The union advantage is also significant in the growing service sector work force, standing at $7 per hour in 2002.[7] On an annual basis this union advantage adds up to thousands of dollars per year for a full-time worker and, significantly, for our pursuit of citizen wealth. This differential has a huge value in and of itself, but can also mean the ability to save and to own a house—the key to a better life for working families.

The last forty years have been a hard time for unions and for workers. The current levels of union membership density reflect the steady, almost inexorable decline of labor power throughout this period. There are many reasons for this decline. Some are outside the control of unions, like the deindustrialization of America and the rise of the unorganized service sector. Other problems are the results of losses on the uneven field of political struggle that saw pro-labor or at least union-neutral laws twisted into unimaginable shapes that then stifled union growth and organizing efforts both deliberately and because of labor's inability to rise to the challenge and adapt. Like any politically governed, membership-based mass institution, unions and their elected leadership naturally respond most quickly to their existing membership and its demands. This has meant that under the employer assault of recent decades in areas like the South where labor organization has remained weak,[8] the membership base lay fallow and undeveloped and was therefore unprepared for the huge demographic and employment shifts of the last forty years.

The legal environment under which unions organize has indeed become an enormous obstacle. An organizer working under the regime of the National Labor Relations Act is something more akin to a workers' paralegal than the prototypical evangelist of the strengths and promises of collective organization and concerted action. The weighting of the system in favor of employers has led to an explosion of unfair labor practices (23,091),[9] firings for union activity (1,373),[10] delays (the average time between filing and election or certification and contract is at least a year),[11] and diminishing rates of success in the organizational process that have led workers to wonder why they should take the risk of organizing for such a thin prospect of rewards. Only 67,501 new workers per year were organized under the National Labor Relations Board (NLRB) in 2006, compared with more than 500,000 organized per year during the 1950s.[12]

Advocates of unions optimistically tout the potential of labor law reform that now, in 2009, seem more likely with the Obama administration and a Democratic Congress than at any other time since the last major reform effort during the Carter administration thirty years ago. The bill attracting most of the attention is the Employee Free Choice Act (EFCA), which showed real life in the U.S. Senate in 2007 and now claims endorsements by President Obama and enough legislators to indicate that passage is possible. EFCA would add higher penalties for firing workers for union activity and a speedier process toward certification, even including the controversial provision for "card check" recognition rather than the bruising, polarizing, and conflicted direct balloting and election process.[13]

After decades working with and for unions as an organizer, however, I am convinced that *any* dependence on a legal regime, either the one now existing under the NLRA or one that might emerge under EFCA or something like it, will not provide real solutions for enrolling sufficient workers into unions to impact the fundamental issues of citizen wealth. If EFCA passes, there may be a period of enthusiasm and union growth, but there will inevitably be a reaction and employer pushback that erodes the gains within a short period of time. To get legislation through Congress with the best intentions and results (as we saw earlier with CRA) is impossible without compromise. For example, simply increasing the penalties for firing pro-union workers will not be sufficient to cause an explosion of union organization. Unless the certification cards can "walk and talk" through an expedited procedure, even with elections similar to those that unions have enjoyed in the province of Quebec and elsewhere, we cannot expect to solve the problems of organization as a key to citizen wealth through legislation. I look forward to eating my hat someday, but I have trouble believing it will be any time soon.

Worker Organizations

I believe that there are other reasons worker organizations can build citizen wealth and organization.

The single largest success over the last generation of labor organizing has—amazingly—been in organizing among the lowest-paid and most marginally employed workers in the emerging service sector: home healthcare and home daycare workers. Perhaps even more amazingly, given the global growth of the "informal" sector of contingent workers, organized labor has achieved its greatest recent success among just such workers, and this has been done off the front pages and in the organizing and political trenches. These efforts led to the organization of more than 500,000 new union members by even the most conservative of estimates, and producing in the process significant increases in wages and benefits for such workers at the very bottom of the employment ladder in our economy. How did this happen? The answer can be found right at the nexus of organizing low-wage workers and combining deep and extensive organization with political muscle and capacity.

The number of home healthcare workers began increasing in the late 1970s, and their numbers exploded in the 1980s because they represented a low-cost alternative to more expensive nursing home or hospital care for the elderly and the infirm. These were workers paid at—or, in many cases, as we were able to prove—below the federal minimum wage. They often had little skilled training and worked under various descriptions as "chore workers," "housekeepers," and unlicensed nursing aides who often helped with light cleaning, shopping, housekeeping, and assisted self-care for elderly clients or those recently discharged from the hospital. These workers usually had no fixed workplace but moved on their own steam using their own vehicles or public transportation to travel from client to client, on assignment from private companies or hospitals while they tried to fill their schedules sufficiently to support themselves and families. Besides such a contingent work experience where the employer was invisible and often confused with the clients themselves, the workers were isolated from each other, sometimes only seeing their "company" and their co-workers when they picked up their checks or went through irregularly scheduled mandatory training sessions.

These lower-wage workers were organizing targets for no union, which is usually the case for low-waged workers because a sustainable labor union business model is hardly based on collecting dues from among those least able to pay them. In ACORN, whose community organizing methodology was street-to-street and door-to-door, organizers slowly began to notice at the end of the 1970s that more of our members were engaged in home health work on a part-time basis while they sought to get off or keep off welfare. We noticed the hard way, because in neighborhood meeting after meeting, members started raising their hands and asking how they could get help on their jobs, and the jobs they described were outside anyone's experience. For a long time leaders and organizers simply looked in the phone book and tried to find out if there were a union that we could refer them to. That strategy would work fine until the next meeting a month or so later, when we would run into the same member who would say, "Hey, no answer," or "The union wasn't interested."

As jobs and income became an increasing focus of ACORN's work in 1978 and 1979, the unions' lack of interest became increasingly obvious. Most unions simply did not have active organizing departments, certainly not on the local union level, and in many cases even on the national or international level. Talking to these unions about why they might want to organize unemployed workers or workers in training programs (like those paid by the Comprehensive Training and Education Act [CETA]) or home health workers was a little like talking to a wall. It was not that they did not care, it was more that they lacked either the capacity or the background or the rationale for the work. As an organization of lower-income members, we tread as fools then where wise men feared to follow,[14] and 1980 found ACORN helping establish and support the United Labor Unions (ULU), an independent union that concentrated on organizing lower-wage workers beginning in Boston, New Orleans, Philadelphia, Detroit, and eventually Chicago.[15] Central to our early work in Boston and later the key to building the local in Chicago was trying to figure out how to organize home healthcare workers into unions.

In Boston, the ULU local focused on nonprofits and for-profit home healthcare agencies with some success, winning several representation elections and in some cases with strikes. The local succeeded in negotiating contracts that moved workers away from the minimum wage and no benefits. In Chicago, the initial focus was similarly on companies under the jurisdiction of the NLRA. The first was called McMaid, which accurately describes the way the company understood its contribution to home healthcare. ULU organizers concentrated on companies like McMaid that used direct distribution of paychecks, giving organizing committee members and organizers an opportunity to meet significant numbers of the workforce as they came to get their checks and moving quickly to organize majorities virtually overnight. The company tried to evade organizing by insisting before the NLRB that it was either not the employer or was a co-employer with its clients, and therefore should be exempt from NLRB jurisdiction.

By 1984, the long-drawn-out efforts to win victories under the NLRA and the legal delays in trying to create bargaining units in home healthcare and among hospitality workers led the United Labor Unions to recognize that we were outgunned in terms of financial, legal, and political resources. The ULU members voted to affiliate with the Service Employees International Union, which seemed supportive of lower-wage worker organizing and rechartered the locals in Boston, New Orleans, and Chicago as SEIU locals.

Later, SEIU Local 880 in Chicago prevailed before the NLRB, with the board holding that McMaid was in fact an employer covered by the NLRA. The NLRB allowed a representation election to go forward among the housekeepers and home health aides, an election the union won handily.[16] In the mid and late 1980s, as Local 880 continued to organize other private-sector home health employers in the Chicago area, hitting the doors in housing projects and working closely with ACORN organizers, they found that some home health aides they were meeting did identical work but were reimbursed directly by the state with no intermediate employer.

Finally, the union began to build a direct membership association of these workers, who were employed by the Illinois Department of Rehabilitation Services (DORS), to sign them up on a monthly dues plan (eventually bank drafts) and elect local chapter leaders to begin lobbying for wage increases and to figure out how to establish organizing rights under Illinois state law. Over a dozen years they made slow but steady progress that built a chapter of thousands of members among DORS workers and meetings that sometimes brought together 200 workers on a Saturday eating donuts and drinking coffee and strategizing about how to get additional clients and work in this unique and individual job.

Organizers involved in the DORS project began to see the potential in other large states like California and Michigan, which were beginning to launch large state-reimbursed home healthcare programs whose workers could be organized in similar ways. New York State had a large home health program largely managed by nonprofits where there had been great success in organizing by unions with SEIU (under John Sweeney when he was president of Local 32 BJ, the building services local in New York City) and Local 1199, the militant hospital workers union.

The problem organizers dealing with these large state-funded programs shared was the same questions originally raised in the private sector by McMaid: Who was the employer? Were these state workers, and if they were, would that mean that they were entitled to the same wages and benefits and other protections enjoyed by public sector workers in those states? Or were they somehow employed by the client and indirectly reimbursed, meaning that they were like independent subcontractors with a list of clients whom they serviced? Perhaps, without realizing it at the time, we had stumbled onto one of the central organizing problems in building income-based wealth for lower-wage, informal sector workers: How can workers create an employer? The question seems perverse. Workers can create unions or other work-based associations, but how could it be possible for workers and their organizations to name a legally responsible employer with whom to bargain? This is (and continues to be) the central problem in stabilizing informal employment around the globe.

Organizers developed strategies to leverage their political clout in certain states where unions still had enough density and power with their deep and long-term organizational support from these workers to create solutions that solidified unions and delivered protections, wages, and benefits to their members. In the case of home-based healthcare and home-based childcare workers, there have been two successful strategies.

The Illinois model was developed over several years by SEIU Local 880 and focused on a multistep organizing program that first achieved dues checkoff (after years of "hand collecting" dues from its members). The local then created meet-and-confer relationships that solidified the dues checkoff program and began to create understandings on procedures and protocols for these informal workers. Local 880 accomplished this while pointedly conceding to the state government that these workers would *not* be classified as state workers and were therefore not eligible for equivalent benefits and wage benefits on the state scale, then, when the opportunity appeared (usually after supporting the winning candidate in the race for governor), winning an executive order that created a bargaining unit, and finally winning legislation that perfected and made permanent the executive order so that future governors could not overturn what had been accomplished. In home healthcare, the Illinois executive order model took more than a dozen years, but SEIU Local 880 was able to convert the home daycare unit in a fraction of that time, having proven to the governor, Rod Blagojevich, that it worked and duplicating the model immediately. The executive order strategy also focused on the fact that the funding streams for both groups of these workers were state reimbursements often matching federal support programs based on income.

The other model was developed in California organizing home healthcare workers there, and could be called the authority model. SEIU used the fact that it was the largest union in the state with significant clout in Sacramento, as well as in a number of the larger counties, to "create an employer" through legislation establishing a public authority that had the power to recognize a union county-by-county and bargain collectively. In California, the most difficult issue was funding the agreements in the always complicated interplay between county finances and state finances, and the necessity of pulling the dollars out of the state and federally reimbursed system to bring all of the pieces together. The funding stream was really the same as that in Illinois for such workers, but because the union leverage moved from the local to the state level, the authorities had to be phased in county by county on a more gradual basis. In California, as in Illinois, there were years, especially in Los Angeles, where members joined, paid dues, and advocated around issues dealing with their wages and working conditions long before the political and organizational planets synchronized sufficiently to allow them to convert that more than a decade of work into victories in some of the largest union representation elections in the U.S. since the 1930s.

Other states and other unions have taken these lessons with the same home-based workers and, with certain adaptations, have built similar victories. For example, ACORN and the Community Labor Organizing Center (CLOC) developed these programs and strategies successfully with the United Federation of Teachers (UFT/AFT) in New York City and the Communication Workers of American (CWA) in New Jersey. These campaigns partnered union resources, commitment, and political clout in these states with our understanding of the workforce and the most efficient method of building community-based unions that were able to deliver worker support as part of the equation. Similar partnerships with SEIU in home-based childcare have been very important, and SEIU has mastered these strategies in ways that have built huge memberships on all of these models in Oregon, Washington, Michigan, Ohio, Pennsylvania, and elsewhere. The American Federation of State, County and Municipal Employees (AFSCME) has followed suit.

These informal workers who were reimbursed by the state and other government agencies but who were not public employees and who were often in an uncertain situation of working as almost independent contractors have joined with community organizations and labor unions to "create employers" and finally win increases in income and benefits and therefore the security that allows for the development of citizen wealth. In doing so over the last decades the unpublicized and unheralded facts remain that informal, almost casual workers have been *the* greatest success story for organized labor in the United States, adding more than half a million members to unions during a period of massive union membership losses. Equally important, these workers in almost every case went from working for the minimum wage, or as close to it as they could be squeezed, with no benefits to moving up the wage ladder and in a number of states (with Illinois as one for leaders here), winning healthcare and other benefits that markedly improve the future for themselves and their families.

The lesson I take from this historic success is not only the pride in accomplishment that we all share in having been a part of one of the few bright spots for workers in this generation, but a belief that

there are alternative and effective models for building worker organizations, if not unions, and that if we are to create citizen wealth,
we need to pursue such alternatives aggressively. At the beginning
of the 21st century I was forced to think about all of this differently
when Andy Stern, as president of SEIU, asked me as a member of the
International's Executive Board to prepare a strategy paper on how to
re-envision labor federations and create a mandate for comprehensive
growth of organized labor, and then present it to the entire board as
an option for the future.

Accepting that challenge with trepidation, I tried to think in a very
different way about what was working, and what was not, and to explore the organizing experiences that might drive different strategies
to achieve worker organization and build citizen wealth. The upshot
was a paper I presented called "Majority Unionism" (with a rudimen-
tary first shot on a PowerPoint presentation) in Seattle in the summer
of 2002 to the full board.[17]

Boiling down my presentation, the core of my argument rested on
several points:

- The demise of organized labor could not be stopped unless
  unions developed new strategies and methodologies that sought
  to create organization and representational status for the majority of the workforce.
- Union strategy over the last thirty to fifty years has too often
  been dominated by the legal environment of the National Labor
  Relations Act. Unrealistic expectations of winning collective bargaining rights have been hugely expensive, not productive, and
  at best are producing only small gains that are reinforcing the
  minority representation status of organized labor in all sectors
  and jurisdictions.
- No strategy would ever work to build "majority unionism" that
  relied on the permission and consent of the employers for their
  workers to have representation and organization. The decision
  and desire of workers should be the starting point for creating
  organization—nothing less and nothing else.
- The numbers of workers in nontraditional, informal, and casual
  work frequently excluded from legal protections and coverage
  under the NLRA are growing in the U.S. and globally. They need

and want organization, though this may not be accessible under the classic collective bargaining regime.

- None of the largest employers that have developed over the last generation of commercial activity are union, especially in the burgeoning service sector, including Wal-Mart, the model for anti-union firms and the largest private-sector employer in the country (and in Canada, Mexico, and, indeed, the world!). A majority unionism strategy would allow workers at such firms to organize in a nontraditional way since other methods have not proved to be effective.

In short, we need to build mass organizations of workers using worker associations that are membership driven and supported by membership dues, and that do not depend for their existence or success on recognition by employers, certification by the state, or the narrow give-and-take of unequal bartering that passes for much of collective bargaining in modern enterprise.

These organizations could produce the kinds of successes that community-based labor experiments, like the ones with home healthcare and home childcare workers, had produced based on novel membership-driven programs. I argued for a labor movement that, for example, would be willing to build and maintain a workers' association of 10 to 20 percent of all Wal-Mart workers (which would still be a membership of over 200,000!). Such associations would represent the workforce on the store floor based on the strength of its organization and would represent the workforce in the public forum, in both cases with programs designed to increase benefits and citizen wealth, rather than meet the requirements of a more narrow legal and bargaining prescription. This point was not unique to Wal-Mart, of course. I offered a list of hundreds of companies. In fact, almost all major employers with more than 50,000 workers established over the last thirty years are non-union, and represent similar opportunities.

Some elements of my argument would almost seem to support building something like an AARP for workers, meaning a very large worker organization that would enroll millions and millions of workers as members and deliver either very specifically on the worksite or more broadly on a menu of interests and even services, with the ability to act as advocates publicly and politically for workers' interests as well.[18] Talk about an AARP for workers is easily disparaged in the current culture of labor, though the macho disdain for such an organizational formation masks some experiments that push the envelope in that direction. Working America, supported and affiliated with the AFL-CIO, is a small-bore, low-threshold way for many workers and their families to join at their homes and be active in supporting the political and legislative aims of organized labor in important states. More interesting, perhaps, is the experience in the United Kingdom of the union called Amicus, which recently formed a global alliance with the United Steelworkers Union. Amicus has millions of members, many of whom joined individually for a host of reasons and in response to different offerings. These members pay dues and collectively identify themselves as a union. In this case the union, like many other unions, is the result of mergers between smaller unions in a variety of jurisdictions that have combined their resources to increase their bargaining power. The UK's Amalgamated Engineering and Electrical Union (AEEU) and Manufacturing, Science, and Finance (MSF) merged to form Amicus, which was joined by Unifi and the Graphical Paper and Media Union (GPMU). Amicus in turn merged with the Transport and General Workers Union to form Unite the Union, which is now the largest union in Britain.[19] The merged experience with the United Steelworkers has already contributed to intensive internal discussions in that union in both Canada and the U.S. about how to reevaluate worker associations in building worker strength and unions. They are building such associations in Canada among Filipino home workers (domestics) in Toronto, taxi drivers in Montreal, and car wash workers in Los Angeles.

Within SEIU, the concept of majority unionism was seen as interesting, but it did not prevail as the union's primary growth strategy.[20] However, there was sufficient interest to create an important experiment to see if Wal-Mart workers would join a workers' association that did not seek a representation election or collective bargaining. In 2005 with support of SEIU, the AFL-CIO, and the United Food and Commercial Workers (UFCW), we initiated a multifaceted program in central Florida around Wal-Mart that engaged the company's growth plans,[21] including Wal-Mart's attempted expansion to India,[22] and the Wal-Mart Workers' Association. In that year over 1000 members joined and paid dues, and almost half of the workers contacted would join. We had organization in more than thirty-five stores, largely in the Orlando and Tampa / St. Petersburg areas, that actively engaged management on store-by-store issues, used the in-house grievance procedure, and won adjustments for their members and other workers on shifts, schedules, wages, and even reinstatements. Despite this initial success, the UFCW was not prepared after the first year to scale up this pilot program. Nevertheless, if workers at such a virulently anti-union company as Wal-Mart were willing to embrace the Wal-Mart Workers' Association without hesitation, joining it and paying their dues, that is strong evidence for the widespread applicability of such a model and methodology in building majority unionism.

The Lessons of Majority Unionism

In short, the majority union proposition for citizen wealth is straightforward and works like this: If workers make more money with increased benefits and job security *because* they are *in* an organization, rather than unorganized, and if such organizations truly are antidotes to poverty because they help increase income and wealth, then regardless of any other reasons (increasing equity, social justice, public participation, and so forth), we need to increase the level of organization among workers if we want to increase citizen wealth. All of the evidence over the last fifty years indicates that the dominant American labor organizing model of representation, certification, and collective bargaining is not succeeding in increasing the membership and density of worker organization.

Furthermore, where labor is recording success and has achieved its greatest growth over the last fifty years has been in the areas where "majority unionism" has been employed. The post-1960s spurt of organization among general public employees and school-based employees was in many cases a situation where worker associations preceded legal procedures and more formal representational regimes. Even now one of the largest worker organizations in the United States is the National Education Association, which has many noncollective bargaining and noncertified organizations of teachers among its 2 million members. The same is true of other unions with large public employee memberships. The public sector is also, not surprisingly if you follow my argument, much better organized with much higher membership and representational density.

The other great success in the last thirty years has been among home-based workers in health and daycare. In most cases this work was pioneered and achieved by patiently employing majority unionism techniques, building member-based worker associations, creating strong community–labor alliances, and building sufficient strength to take advantage of eventual opportunities and leverage on the political side.

To achieve increased citizen wealth for lower-wage workers, we have to use models and methods such as majority unionism that lower the bar and eliminate the barriers to associational activity and self-representation of workers themselves. If worker organizations rely on employer decisions or on a system that is dominated by employers, they cannot hope to deliver the increases in income, benefits, and protection that create citizen wealth.

While there are still unions in the United States and before they are obliterated completely, they need to begin thinking outside of the NLRA and collective bargaining cage. We've been there, done that, and that deal has been taken off the table. There's no reason to pretend those times are coming back, even if new legislation such as the Employee Free Choice Act is passed.

In order to address workers' wages and wealth, we need to open up the throttle, go into overdrive, and fashion organizations and strategies large enough to appeal to and enable the participation of the vast majority of American workers, especially lower-wage workers. And we need to have done that by yesterday.

Part II
Protecting and Advancing Citizen Wealth

6

Making Earned Income Tax Credits Work for Workers

There are programs that are designed to increase income and security for working and other families at the bottom of the ladder. The Earned Income Tax Credit (EITC) for working families is certainly the most popular, and perhaps the most effective, of these programs, but some other income maintenance and support programs still exist for low-income families.

But despite the intentions of such programs, there paradoxically continues to be a significant income gap that translates into families being poorer than they should be and available dollars being unspent to address the issues of income and wealth. Without full participation of all eligible families in these programs we are not taking advantage of existing authorizations and appropriations, and programs are missing the benchmarks of success that they should achieve. Borrowing a term from Lyndon Johnson's time, we need to join in a campaign to achieve *maximum eligible participation* where all families entitled to income support benefits actually receive them. (We will focus on this campaign at more length in Chapter 9.)

The hard problem should be creating programs. The easy part should be getting participation in the programs. This mismatch demands a solution because it translates into billions of dollars of lost income and the real difference between destitution and a semblance of economic security for many citizens.

EITC

Initially passed by Congress in 1975, and made permanent in 1978, the Earned Income Tax Credit is one of the only programs that federal administrations, both Republican and Democratic, joined by heavy support in Congress when controlled by either party, believe is an effective response to poverty. None of this should be surprising, because the EITC is primarily designed to subsidize lower-wage work, particularly the kind of contingent work so common in the service industry that pays a nominal wage at the federal minimum standard but delivers irregular and part-time hours and therefore doesn't provide enough income for either a secure livelihood or any prospect of citizen wealth. By supporting lower-wage work and informal labor in this way, capped near the level that would yield an income delivered by full-time hours at the federal minimum wage with the benefit tailing off after reaching that amount, the EITC is a tax-based subsidy for low-wage work that business and politicians can love, and that lower-income families can struggle to access and sustain.

If this is the largest anti-poverty program in the United States, let us first try to get a solid grasp on its reach and range:

- In tax year 2003 the EITC was received by 19.2 million tax filers at a cost of $34 billion.[1]
- The average credit per family in 2003 was $1784.[2]
- In tax year 2006, qualifying families with two or more children received up to $4536 and families with one child received up to $2747. Workers with no dependent children received a maximum of $412 from the federal EITC.[3]
- The popularity of the program has led an additional sixteen states to offer "add-on" EITCs.[4]
- The annual gross income (AGI) for single filers with one child was $30,338 in 2004; for single filers with two or more children it was $34,458.[5]
- Income received from other sources of citizen wealth (interest, rent, dividends, etc.) could not be larger than $2650 in 2004.[6]
- About 75 percent of EITC is paid to tax filers who are single heads of household.[7]
- Some 61 percent of EITC is paid to filers with two or more children.[8]

Despite the bipartisan support for the EITC, former President Bill Clinton is correct when he takes credit for a significant expansion of the program. During his administration expenditures on the program increased from around $10 billion a year to close to $35 billion a year, and have not exceeded that total subsequently.[9]

This expansion in the EITC dwarfs other major income supplement programs administered by the federal government, including Temporary Assistance for Needy Families (TANF) and Food Stamps. In 2003 it looked like this:[10]

Program	Cost/Billions	Families/Millions	Average Benefit/Month
EITC	$33.4	19.6	$142
TANF	$24.5	2.1	$351
Food Stamps	$21.0	7.4	$174

Besides being an efficient program that provides incentives to work, EITC enjoys wide and deep support for other reasons. Working families in many cases are not eligible for existing federal healthcare programs, and studies of EITC indicate that 20 percent of the money received through EITC payments ends up paying for healthcare.[11] Studies have also shown that lower-income working families are disproportionately inclined to spend their money in their own communities and cities, so there is a multiplier effect that keeps and expands the benefit of the EITC dollars within the local economy. An important study done by the Nashville Wealth Building Alliance during 2005 indicated that EITC multiplier effects added $81.8 million to the local economy.[12] EITC is quite simply a program that just keeps providing benefits at every level.

For all of the ideological and political support for EITC the program still has some drawbacks. One of the most glaring is the continued inability of the program to achieve full participation after thirty years of ineffective efforts. Much of the responsibility for this shortfall in participation can be laid at the feet of the Internal Revenue Service (IRS), which administers the program.

The IRS is unparalleled at receiving payments from business and families. No one can beat the agency for its ability to open the mail, review the returns, and get the money to the bank. It is also excellent at doing outreach when it is part of its core mission, like collecting taxes from your deadbeat, scofflaw cousin or reminding you that you miscalculated in some itsy-bitsy way—but forget about asking the IRS to put together a program that figures out how to achieve full participation of eligible families in EITC.

Estimates continue to vary on the number of families that qualify for but do not receive EITC and, correspondingly, on the amount of money being left on the table and not being used to move more families and children toward citizen wealth. However, credible research suggests that 25 percent of families who are eligible for EITC do not claim it,[13] which is far too many. These are real families. The numbers missing benefits would then be about 3 million families who are not receiving $3.5 billion in EITC support.[14] Importantly, Hispanic families are among the groups where participation in EITC is lowest.[15] States like California are particularly hard-hit, with average participation percentages that do not exceed 70 percent among Latinos. Language is obviously a barrier, along with a reluctance to take on unfamiliar systems and hostile environments. African American families also have a lower-than-average participation rate, and all of this swells in specific urban census tracts and zip codes where eligibility is extremely high and participation rates are inadequate.

Table 4 shows the benefits by state in 2007, as estimated by the ACORN Centers and the ACORN Financial Justice Center, if we had achieved full participation in the EITC program.

The IRS's response to this problem is passive and half-hearted. When it receives a return from a filer whom its computers indicate is eligible for EITC, the IRS reportedly sends a notice to the filer saying that he or she is eligible and needs to apply—rather than making an automatic adjustment and correction the way the agency would do on an error made by a middle-income filer.[16] Language barriers should not be mountains to climb, yet the IRS has seemingly made them Himalayan. Similarly, the concentrations of eligible families should make increasing participation easier to achieve because of the very density involved, yet the IRS has refused to meet this challenge. These failures make no sense in building citizen wealth or combating wage-based poverty.

EITC Campaigns

Several years ago Luz Vega-Marquiz, president of the Marguerite Casey Foundation, along with Drummond Pike, president and CEO of the San Francisco–based Tides Foundation, challenged me during a lunchtime conversation to stop talking about the EITC participation gap and devise a program to deal with it—and pledged that her foundation would support that program for a year. Her challenge led to some major ACORN pilot programs to field-test whether a concentrated outreach program would really produce results. The programs included door-to-door home visits in zip code areas where ACORN research had determined there were high numbers of eligible families but low levels of participation.

ACORN chose as the pilot cities San Antonio (to see if we could increase the low participation among Hispanics), New Orleans (focusing on the heavily African American 9th Ward), and Miami (in a mixed Latino, Caribbean, and African American area). The results were shocking, though not surprising. Participation rates skyrocketed as a result of the outreach programs. ACORN also organized free tax preparation centers in these areas to help increase participation, and in one tax season these centers became the largest EITC tax preparers in all three cities. In New Orleans the number of applicants in the city doubled as a result of the ACORN program. Needless to say, both ACORN and the Marguerite Casey Foundation were ecstatic and went on to deepen their partnership in the areas of financial justice around tax issues for a number of years with great results.

EITC has demonstrated tremendous and indisputable effectiveness, but it still fails to realize its full potential. We need a national crusade to achieve full enrollment in this and other eligible programs so that we achieve *maximum eligible participation*. The IRS is a perfect example where the core competency, experience, and budget necessary to achieve widespread outreach among lower-income workers and their families are simply lacking, resulting in inadequate participation after all these years. The IRS may be very efficient at delivering services to existing participants or members, but it has failed to think innovatively and effectively when it comes to developing new models and paradigms to solve problems in participation that are now decades old. We need to either create a new capacity and install a new attitude within the IRS if it is to continue to administer such a vital program, or we

Table 4 Benefits of Full EITC Participation, 2007

State	Total Returns	EITC Recipients	Total EITC Dollars Received	Average Amount per Household	15% EITC Unclaimed	Amount Unclaimed
Alabama	1,860,240	481,255	$1.011 Billion	$2,101	72,188	$151.7 Million
Alaska	329,743	38,658	$59.8 Million	$1,548	5,799	$9 Million
Arizona	2,287,509	393,020	$721.3 Million	$1,835	58,953	$108.1 Million
Arkansas	1,108,357	275,719	$539 Million	$1,955	41,358	$80.8 Million
California	14,581,518	2,377,010	$4.271 Billion	$1,797	356,552	$640.6 Million
Colorado	2,037,777	259,429	$426.7 Million	$1,645	38,914	$64 Million
Connecticut	1,630,560	164,999	$267.7 Million	$1,622	24,750	$40.2 Million
Delaware	384,861	56,343	$99.7 Million	$1,769	8,451	$14.9 Million
DC	265,635	47,819	$83.3 Million	$1,741	7,173	$12.5 Million
Florida	7,835,964	1,555,922	$2.864 Billion	$1,841	233,388	$429.6 Million
Georgia	3,692,406	842,445	$1.705 Billion	$2,024	126,367	$255.8 Million
Hawaii	587,220	85,177	$137.3 Million	$1,612	12,777	$20.6 Million
Idaho	578,871	99,738	$174.2 Million	$1,746	14,961	$26.1 Million
Illinois	5,603,181	842,855	$1.546 Billion	$1,834	126,428	$231.9 Million
Indiana	2,791,278	424,907	$745.8 Million	$1,755	63,736	$111.9 Million
Iowa	1,310,456	168,252	$274.3 Million	$1,630	25,238	$41.1 Million
Kansas	1,194,662	173,087	$298.7 Million	$1,726	25,963	$44.8 Million
Kentucky	1,719,401	337,492	$599.6 Million	$1,776	50,624	$89.9 Million
Louisiana	1,762,935	509,787	$1.102 Billion	$2,161	76,468	$165.2 Million
Maine	609,345	85,240	$135.7 Million	$1,592	12,786	$20.4 Million
Maryland	2,542,923	337,345	$583.6 Million	$1,730	50,602	$87.5 Million
Massachu- setts	2,978,758	303,861	$482.7 Million	$1,589	45,579	$72.4 Million
Michigan	4,427,936	639,875	$1.140 Billion	$1,782	95,981	$171 Million
Minnesota	2,356,778	255,289	$402.6 Million	$1,577	38,293	$60.4 Million
Mississippi	1,131,541	366,904	$787.4 Million	$2,146	55,036	$118.1 Million
Missouri	2,524,646	432,142	$770.7 million	$1,783	64,821	$115.6 Million
Montana	429,841	72,293	$120.1 Million	$1,662	10,844	$18 Million

Table 4 Continued

State	Total Returns	EITC Recipients	Total EITC Dollars Received	Average Amount per Household	15% EITC Unclaimed	Amount Unclaimed
Nebraska	789,358	108,192	$184.6 Million	$1,707	16,229	$27.7 Million
Nevada	1,045,638	157,890	$269.7 Million	$1,708	23,684	$40.5 Million
New Hampshire	632,722	61,787	$95.4 Million	$1,544	9,268	$14.3 Million
New Jersey	3,998,031	480,951	$838.4 Million	$1,743	72,143	$125.8 Million
New Mexico	803,954	194,662	$359 Million	$1,844	29,199	$53.9 Million
New York	8,381,665	1,449,138	$2.598 Billion	$1,793	217,371	$389.7 Million
North Carolina	3,656,576	747,125	$1.410 Billion	$1,888	112,069	$211.6 Million
North Dakota	300,451	39,058	$63.4 Million	$1,624	5,859	$9.5 Million
Ohio	5,344,064	781,146	$1.381 Billion	$1,768	117,172	$207.1 Million
Oklahoma	1,427,976	306,956	$573 Million	$1,867	46,043	$85.9 Million
Oregon	1,544,715	219,734	$362.4 Million	$1,649	32,960	$54.4 Million
Pennsylvania	5,709,561	765,233	$1.284 Billion	$1,678	114,785	$192.6 Million
Rhode Island	488,730	64,292	$110.7 Million	$1,721	9,644	$16.6 Million
South Carolina	1,796,609	422,376	$814.3 Million	$1,928	63,356	$122.1 Million
South Dakota	356,609	54,720	$91.3 Million	$1,668	8,208	$13.7 Million
Tennessee	2,553,641	542,004	$1.011 Billion	$1,866	81,301	$151.7 Million
Texas	9,142,003	2,169,274	$4.449 Billion	$2,051	325,391	$667.3 Million
Utah	963,949	137,907	$241.9 Million	$1,754	20,686	$36.3 Million
Vermont	303,022	37,844	$56.7 Million	$1,498	5,677	$8.5 Million
Virginia	3,378,130	485,636	$857.4 Million	$1,765	72,845	$128.6 Million
Washington	2,766,982	350,084	$584 Million	$1,668	52,513	$87.6 Million
West Virginia	739,550	143,701	$245.6 Million	$1,709	21,555	$36.8 Million
Wisconsin	2,577,577	292,566	$479.2 Million	$1,638	43,885	$71.9 Million
Wyoming	238,281	33,071	$53.7 million	$1,625	4,961	$8.1 Million
Total for All States	127,504,136	21,672,210	$39.8 Billion	$1,794	3,250,832	$5.964 Billion

Total EITC Dollars Available for All States $45.7 Billion

Source: Jeff Karlson and Diné Butler, "EITC Participation Chart" (St. Paul, Minn.: ACORN Financial Justice Center).

need to transfer that capacity and responsibility to another agency to get the job done finally and done fully.

In the same ways that, when thwarted by an immovable object in federal administrations and Congress around living wages, community groups were forced to become irresistible forces at the local level to achieve needed reforms, so through the ACORN Centers (formerly ACORN Tax and Benefit Centers) and the ACORN Financial Justice Center, we have been trying to convince local states and governments to engage more fully in the process of creating maximum eligible participation in EITC and other programs. Normally, one would think that raw self-interest and irrefutable community economic benefits alone would trump any ambiguous feelings toward poor working families and convince governors and mayors to spend some to make lots in this area. But bureaucracies being what they are, sometimes the sell is a hard one, no matter how compelling the logic.

Ironically, given that the program is administered by the IRS, significant time and resources go to dealing with misfiling and payments to filers who turn out to be ineligible,[17] but little or nothing to the opposite: outreach. Clearly, I am not advocating misspending government money, and I absolutely support making sure that the money is fully utilized for all eligible participants. However, the imbalance in the efforts to catch the poor making errors rather than to ensure that all eligible families participate seems misdirected. I would argue that no more should be spent on punitive enforcement mechanisms than is dedicated to effective outreach and participation programs, so that the mission of EITC is realized rather than continually subverted. In his appearance before the U.S. House of Representatives, Leonard E. Burman of the Urban Institute stated, "[The IRS] estimate[s] the EITC compliance gap [estimated total taxes due but not collected] at $7.8 billion in 1998, about 0.5 percent of revenues and about 2.8 percent of the total tax gap. But EITC enforcement accounts for 3.8 percent of total enforcement budget in 2003. Indeed, the IRS has requested a 68.5 percent increase in its EITC enforcement budget, while increasing other enforcement by only 3.3 percent. In fact, the increase in EITC enforcement would account for 45 percent of all new compliance dollars (Internal Revenue Service 2003). On its face, this seems like an inefficient way to spend scarce compliance resources."[18]

EITC is also one of the few programs that can drive not only income but also wealth. Studies show that lower-income families have the same propensity to save as other families, but often lack the opportunity represented by cash in excess of survival requirements.[19] Not surprisingly, the same studies show that tax refunds are the portion of income that drives much of savings for lower-income families.[20] There is therefore a huge opportunity that comes not only from fuller EITC participation but also from programs that receive public and private support that could encourage savings. Matched and incentivized accounts like Individual Development Accounts (IDAs), seeded by even small amounts of money diverted to savings or investments from tax and EITC returns, could have magnified benefits in wealth creation, so every cent of these billions of dollars is very, very important.

Incidentally, IDAs have real potential and have generated a lot of excitement since they appeared on the scene around 1999,[21] and many believe that they could offer a huge boost in citizen wealth and asset building. Over the last decade, though, the expenditures have been trivial, and estimates vary on the number of IDA accounts nationally. The highest estimate is 15,000 accounts, with a total of 20,000 including those who have opened and then closed accounts having reached the savings objective or purchase goal. Twenty-one states have initiated IDA programs,[22] with almost all of the rest passing some form of IDA but not funding it. A large part of the enthusiasm for getting this done undoubtedly lies with statewide asset-building coalitions. Where they exist, such coalitions have drawn together an impressive array of nonprofits, community-based institutions including community development banks, and private foundations.[23] Unfortunately, not enough of the coalitions have gotten active and excited participation from financial institutions yet, and that speaks to the underlying issues as well.

A look at the list shows that the best of the bunch seem to be in Arkansas and Oregon in terms of the level of matching funds, the level of assets allowed to be built, and the wide discretionary purposes for which a family can spend their savings. For the most part, appropriations for most of the programs that do exist come from excess or allocated TANF funds. Most of the eligible families are TANF eligible as well, so this has not become a robust program to date despite the warm feeling that many have expressed in its general direction. The real action has been much more tentative, and the reason may lie in the fact that someone somewhere would actually have to spend money to create the match, and without the match these are just passbook savings accounts.

Importantly, though, the IDA savings and matched asset itself are *not* counted at all as part of the asset test for eligibility, and this could be a real breakthrough if it extended not just to IDAs but to a whole array of citizen wealth–building measures. The whole asset test bugaboo for lower-income and working families works profoundly against citizen wealth and creates a huge disincentive for families to build any wealth nest egg. Asset tests are policies that need to be rethought because they make citizen wealth creation a program with adverse, if not punitive, consequences in terms of lost or potentially lost benefits from other programs and entitlements.

EITC Lessons

The problem of wealth driven by EITC seems similar to the problem of full citizen voting rights stymied by cumbersome registration requirements. Rather than creating automatic registration systems similar to those Richard Cloward and Frances Fox Piven have advocated or based on the work of many of us that led to successful motor-voter legislation,[24] we still have a system that is time consuming, expensive, prone to mistakes, and premised on a "gotcha" regime of catching mistakes and trying to criminalize voting.

This kind of program acts as a restraint to voter participation, because lower-income voters are not interested in "making mistakes" in voting or registration that could have criminal or civil penalties leading to cutbacks on entitlements, eviction from public housing, and public ridicule. A similar lack of a "welcoming" attitude at the IRS leads me to be anything but surprised that when the IRS "notices" that a lower-income filer might be eligible, the intimidation of the paperwork and the service itself is a barrier to maximum eligible participation.

Studies of registration and voting indicate that the actual impact of mistakes in registration is almost completely trivial. A bad registration does not convert into a bad vote. Someone may register as Mickey Mouse, but everyone knows that there is only one Mickey Mouse and that he votes in either Anaheim or Orlando, depending on the season and the election. Most of the reported problems with registration do not reflect people trying to vote illegitimately.[25] Some countries, such as Brazil and Australia, enforce mandatory voting by the entire electorate—which, importantly, also means the poor. In Brazil pictures of the candidates and the parties show on touch screens to make exercising the franchise welcoming to even the illiterate. In America, where less than 50 percent of eligible voters vote even in presidential contests other than in exceptional circumstances, we gain none of the efficiencies and benefits of full registration, yet spend tens of millions both on the registration process and on the bureaucracy to enable and check registration on the government side of the window.

But here is my real point. In program after program, whether EITC or voter registration, we are seeing ideological and narrow political complaints trump real delivery of benefits, either economic or citizenship, to eligible families. Why has the idea not become a commonplace that citizens and society as a whole benefit more by full participation in all social programs, including EITC and other entitlements, as well as full access and voting franchise (as opposed to the existing registration system) despite the occasional problems and abuses? Why instead are we celebrating the achievement of "voluntary inequities" under the cumbersome enrollment systems that currently exist? Everyone in America is better off if all boats rise. The costs of the effort to prevent a few stragglers from boarding dwarf the benefits of getting entitled citizens into participation. This imbalance is corrosive and must be changed.

A Note on Citizen Wealth for Immigrants

In the perverse psyche of today's American society, there is no getting around the fact that we have to deal with immigrants, particularly new immigrants with uncertain status, as a separate and distinct part of the problem of creating citizen wealth. In some ways none of this is totally new, though it has become *muy complicado* in the years since September 11, 2001, and especially because recent congressional legislation has become starkly punitive in slapping back at immigrants and restricting benefits.

But all that is part of the national argument and debate, so without getting in over our heads, let us first get a sense of the real facts so we can stand on solid ground:

- Rough estimates are that there are now 12 to 15 million undocumented immigrants in the U.S.
- Since August 22, 1996, even legal immigrants arriving in the United States have in most cases been barred from accessing Medicaid or SCHIP health programs, such as Medicare, for a five-year period. This rule was changed only recently by the incoming Obama administration.
- The same barrier applies to most of the rest of the benefits we have been discussing, like Food Stamps, low-income home energy assistance, and other public support programs where both legal—and undocumented—immigrants are barred for five years.
- Immigrants who work, whether legal or undocumented, pay taxes.
- Immigrants are eligible for and entitled to EITC benefits.
- In some cases states are even more restrictive than the federal government in denying assistance and support to immigrants.

EITC is still the one program carrying the load in immigrant communities—which is not surprising considering the fact that it is work-based and that many immigrants, even undocumented immigrants, are here in the U.S. *especially* to work. An interesting report done by the Brookings Institution researchers in 2000 provided some snapshots of the EITC "community" among immigrants.[26] They found the following:

- In the 5 percent of the nation's zip codes where over half of all foreign-born people live, they found that the concentrations of the foreign-born were in New York, California, and Texas, and that 20 percent of them had incomes below the poverty line.
- They found that 21 percent of families in these "high-immigrant" communities were receiving EITC (compared to 15 percent nationally).
- Tax filers from these areas claimed $6.7 billion (20 percent of total EITC dollars claimed in 2000). By 2002, that number had risen to $7.8 billion.
- Lower-income working families were more likely to use a paid tax preparer to file their taxes compared to those in other communities, yet they were also less likely to try to get a refund

anticipation loan, both of which are interesting and important findings.

- Communities with more moderate concentrations of immigrants (2 to 13 percent) seem to have lower EITC participation rates than communities with especially high concentrations, or, conversely, especially low numbers of immigrants. In short, it seems to "take a village," which also argues for extensive, targeted outreach in such areas as an effective strategy for increasing EITC participation, which is consistent with our entire argument as well as putting the burden on similar outreach to spread the word where families are more diffuse and scattered.

Among undocumented immigrants the Tax Foundation has noted that many are increasingly attempting to file tax returns under ITIN numbers. Between 2004 and 2005 there was a 40 percent increase in such filings reported by the IRS, with as many as 1.4 million returns using such numbers. This obviously presents a problem for EITC. If you do not have a social security number (or at least an ITIN), you cannot file a return, so no matter how hard you might have worked and how little you might have been paid, therefore making you eligible, you will not get a tax credit or cash payment, because you literally do not exist in the system. This contribution by undocumented immigrants who will never collect social security benefits is an important factor in financing the entire social security system.[27]

7

Guarding Tax Refunds and Combatting High Prices

I have tried to forcefully introduce the concept that the job is unfinished unless we have full participation in programs creating citizen wealth, but the primary rule of asset building has to be that we cannot allow anyone or anything to steal or suck away the precious dollars that lower-income and working families must have to achieve economic security. In creating citizen wealth, a good offense has to be coupled with an equally powerful defense. There's no sense in doing all of the work to put money in people's pockets and then allowing those same pockets to be picked clean. We need a citizen wealth regime that allows us to take two steps forward without taking one step back.

When we looked at entitlement programs like EITC we saw that we have to be extremely vigilant about potentially predatory products and pricing like refund anticipation loans (RALs) offered by tax preparers, who should be the agents helping families receive the benefits. There are also some problems we can predict that can cripple fragile family economies because their income and assets are not elastic enough to handle the pressures caused by inflation in the price of necessities like food and fuel, yet surprisingly there are no programs in place that protect lower-income families from the global economic tsunamis that overwhelm the slender dikes built by few assets, limited income, and marginal wealth. Nonetheless, we need to shore up family defenses in all of these areas. Let's look at how both of these problems are threatening efforts to create citizen wealth at the bottom.

Refund Anticipation Loans

Private tax preparers offering refund anticipation loans divert huge revenues from lower-income, working families. They deliver slightly faster refunds to many of these families—both those receiving EITC, where the case is perhaps even more despicable, and other working families, who see tapping into their tax refunds as one of their few sources of "savings" available on an annual basis. The IRS for too long has allowed access to EITCs to be functionally privatized through tax preparers and has turned its attention away from the predatory scandal represented by RALs and similar products. There are currently some signs of positive change in this area, but change has been slow in coming. There have also been major efforts to curtail RALs by ACORN, as well as other financial justice coalitions that are attempting to eliminate RALs from the market or create a less predatory price structure.

An ACORN Financial Justice Center report in 2004 documented this problem thoroughly and in sobering fashion.[1] The ACORN report showed that the RALs were indeed sucking away money from EITC and other working families who depended on their tax refunds:

- The total costs of RALs could range from $180 to over $250, taking about 10 percent of the average EITC return.
- In the 2002 filing season 12.7 million consumers paid $1.14 billion in loan fees.
- Alarmingly, 55 percent of RAL borrowers were EITC recipients, so this was a program preying on the poorest tax filers.[2]

RALs are not a value-added product in the tax preparation industry. Their existence is tied to the fact that these companies understand that some lower-income and working families depend on their tax refunds desperately enough that they are either unable to wait the extra week or two for the IRS to deliver their refund, or they do not have bank accounts or others means to facilitate electronic transfer from the IRS on the quickest basis possible. In exchange for speed and with the conviction that the return is expected and secure, the preparer (and the banks that are lending them the money) advance the amount of the refund so the filer has it in hand immediately rather than having to wait. This convenience is predatory, since it depends on families being desperate enough to be willing to pay what have historically been near-usurious rates of interest and fees to have the money up front.

The main banks financing these RALs were HSBC, JPMorgan Chase, and Santa Barbara Bank and Trust. They shared about $690 million by some estimates.[3] There was plenty of fruit to divide from this poisoned tree, and Table 5 gives a pretty good look at the take from RALs.

In 2003, ACORN decided to go directly after the major tax preparers on RALs and other issues that were impacting our members. This industry is very fragmented according to the ACORN Financial Justice Center. Three big companies control about one-third of the tax preparation business, and the rest of the business is atomized into thousands of mom-and-pop tax prep offices that open and close with the tax season. The biggest by far, though, was H&R Block. We concluded quickly that it made sense to go after Block to see if the company would bend, and then use that settlement as a pattern to see if we could leverage the industry into changing its predatory practices.

At this point, ACORN had the membership size and the geographic range to engage national targets in a way that was unique among community groups. We began with a series of direct actions targeting H&R Block at the end of 2003 to signal what the tax season could mean for the company under a full city-by-city assault. We ramped up by early to mid-January 2004 with reports and actions office by office. By the time we got a call from Block representatives indicating that the company was willing to negotiate, we had done over 400 actions in forty-three cities around the country.[4]

Before our campaign started we had not fully appreciated how effective our timing was. We discovered that there are huge peaks and valleys in tax preparation work. An incredible proportion of the total returns for a company like H&R Block, which does 19.9 million returns, are performed in two periods. The first comes between the third week of January and the middle of February, when most people receive their W-2s, while the second is the final push between the last week of March and the middle of April.[5] By gearing up hard at the very beginning of tax season H&R Block could weigh soberly whether or not it was willing to endure the ACORN campaign and its impact on its business and brand throughout the season or was better served by negotiating with us. The second thing we learned, once we began

Table 5 Refund Anticipation Loans and RAL Fees, by State

State	Number of RALs	RAL Fees	State	Number of RALs	RAL Fees
Alabama	306,372	$36,764,640	Montana	24,334	$2,920,080
Alaska	17,090	$32,050,800	Nebraska	36,977	$4,437,240
Arizona	167,917	$20,150,040	Nevada	104,308	$12,516,960
Arkansas	171,657	$20,598,840	New Hampshire	28,290	$3,394,800
California	742,202	$89,064,240	New Jersey	241,212	$28,945,440
Colorado	98,534	$11,824,080	New Mexico	67,996	$8,159,520
Connecticut	73,301	$8,796,120	New York	537,067	$64,448,040
Delaware	29,286	$3,514,320	North Carolina	517,081	$62,049,720
D.C.	27,871	$3,344,520	North Dakota	12,337	$1,480,440
Florida	721,335	$86,560,200	Ohio	440,443	$52,853,160
Georgia	517,468	$62,096,160	Oklahoma	155,206	$18,624,720
Hawaii	26,997	$3,239,640	Oregon	63,590	$7,630,800
Idaho	27,222	$3,266,640	Pennsylvania	338,898	$40,667,760
Illinois	444,780	$53,373,600	Rhode Island	28,051	$3,366,120
Indiana	269,383	$32,325,960	South Carolina	282,566	$33,907,920
Iowa	62,511	$7,501,320	South Dakota	24,790	$2,974,800
Kansas	71,048	$8,525,760	Tennessee	359,952	$43,194,240
Kentucky	202,934	$24,352,080	Texas	1,195,274	$143,432,880
Louisiana	299,424	$35,930,880	Utah	41,937	$5,032,440
Maine	28,580	$3,429,600	Vermont	9,835	$1,180,200
Maryland	175,080	$21,009,600	Virginia	282,618	$33,914,160
Massachusetts	97,568	$11,708,160	Washington	153,012	$18,361,440
Michigan	314,404	$37,728,480	West Virginia	77,195	$9,263,400
Minnesota	68,145	$8,177,400	Wisconsin	93,731	$11,247,720
Mississippi	247,705	$29,724,600	Wyoming	15,735	$1,888,200
Missouri	207,970	$24,956,400	U.S. Total	10,549,219	$1,265,906,280

Source: ACORN Financial Justice Center, "Refund Anticipation Loan Costs" (St. Paul, Minn.: ACORN Financial Justice Center, 2006).

negotiations, is that the relationship between H&R Block and HSBC, as its RALs banker, meant that there was an acute appreciation of the value of moving quickly to negotiations rather than enduring a prolonged and costly battle over several years—a conclusion that HSBC had drawn as a result of the Household Finance campaign.

In short, the company quickly sued for peace, and even more rapidly agreed to unconditional negotiations in New Orleans with ACORN national leadership and staff and a top team led by Block's chief operating officer. The speed is evident from the fact that the first session took place on February 2, 2004.

The first session was interesting and began with as transparent an opening as any negotiations I have ever led, when we were asked whether Block was the target "because we are the biggest or because we are the worst." We quickly answered, "Because you are the biggest, and you could be the best." From there the game was on. We concentrated on predatory practices, disclosures particularly around the costs of RALs, and other issues. Unlike many firms that we had engaged, the company never asked us as a quid pro quo of the negotiations that we cease actions against them, which was novel. Fortunately, we had enough experience to understand that we either had to continue actions or to negotiate in good faith, but we could not push both strategies at the same time, and so ceased the actions based on the progress we had made toward an agreement.

No doubt this helped make subsequent sessions move apace, with another face-to-face meeting held on March 5, this time in Block's training center in Kansas City, then a conference call session on March 15, another conference call on March 30, and then, on April 23, the critical final session in Kansas City at Block's world headquarters. This meeting culminated in a final agreement that pleased everyone on both sides of the table, and gave us the precedent we needed to move on the rest of the tax preparation industry.

Critical to the agreement was the fact that H&R Block dropped its fees from the RALs. We estimated that this one reduction saved $200 million for tax filers during the next year.[6] H&R Block also convinced us that its CEO and chairman believed that RALs were never going to be a permanent part of the marketplace for lower-income taxpayers, but that the company could not "unilaterally disarm" from offering them as long as its top competitors continued to push them heavily.

We already had the next largest, Jackson Hewitt, in our sights, with Liberty Tax Services, the third largest tax-prep firm, right behind. This additional information was all we needed to convince us that we were right on target.

H&R Block thus set the pattern for subsequent industry agreements. Jackson Hewitt began negotiating by late 2004, and after a few actions and dustups we had the agreement locked down in principle by the end of the 2005 tax season. More of this company's operations were franchises, so there was a longer phase-out of the company fees for RALs, but they were unsustainable once H&R Block dropped its RAL fees.

Liberty Tax Services ran almost all of its business through franchises, and the company was actually run by John Hewitt himself, who had sold his namesake, gotten around the noncompete clause by opening up franchises for Liberty in Canada, and relocated in Virginia Beach once he could franchise again in the U.S. He was a serial entrepreneur and quite a character, and as such an easier meeting and a harder sell on the advantages of negotiating under the pattern agreement. An action by several hundred ACORN members at Liberty's headquarters during the heart of the 2005 tax season after a successful face-to-face meeting in February of that year went awry at the building's door, leading to a melee covered extensively by local television and hundreds of arrests, many of which scooped up ACORN members who had never gotten off the bus. Liberty filed a SLAPP suit (a "strategic lawsuit against public participation") against ACORN as a result, and it was a mess for months.

Craig Robbins, ACORN's deputy field director and regional director for the Northeast, finally put the pressure on for a settlement by coordinating an on-the-ground canvass in Virginia Beach targeting the company's predatory products and practices in its home territory, which helped convince the company that there would be no peace without a settlement. By January 2006, Jordan Ash, ACORN Financial Justice Center's director, and I were meeting at a seafood restaurant on the Potomac in Washington, D.C., with company representatives, who finally agreed to a deal based on the H&R Block pattern.

RALs are a pernicious product because, unfortunately, lower-income members are desperate for their tax refunds and are therefore frequently willing to pay an outrageous premium to get that money a few days or weeks before the IRS can send it. The willing compliance of the victim is, after all, part of what makes the situation predatory. This is not simply a case of a customer paying an extra dollar or two to get a book bought on Amazon shipped a couple of days faster by UPS than could be done by the U.S. Postal Service, because the interest rates for RALs are frequently in the triple digits. The companies understood this situation thoroughly. No matter how we negotiated the disclosures they would need to make, from lists of fees on a computer screen to giant posters at Jackson Hewitt that would show that the effective interest rates and charges could sometimes reach as much as 250 percent, none of that seemed to change the market for the RAL product. Desperate is desperate, and people were paying out money that they did not have in their pockets yet, so it did not *feel* like it hurt the same way.

Nonetheless, our work and that of countless others were all combining, by small steps and big leaps, to make RALs less tenable in the marketplace. The problem was no longer a well-kept secret, but increasingly a low-grade national scandal that defined a rip-off.

This situation is possibly the worst of its kind, because it diverted one of the largest sources of potential savings and citizen wealth creation for lower-income and working families, and it continues to be a problem that has to be solved, no matter how many other reforms might be won from tax preparers, both large and small.

Inflation: The High Cost of Food and Fuel

The increasing concern around global warming and the potential carbon credits that are one strategy for incentivizing more responsible corporate behavior are intriguing, but such actions need to ensure that they do not create what are in effect regressive taxes on citizen wealth for families at the bottom in the form of higher prices for gasoline, public transit, utilities, fuel oil, and other necessities. The last increase in EITC benefits came as a result of a discussion of a similar BTU tax, and future debates are likely to lead to similar measures. We need to align the interests of the majority constituency (low- and moderate-income families) with planetary sustainability, but that requires a reorientation of balanced consequences around policy changes. The soaring prices of fuel that marked much of 2008, even though falling during the ensuing recession, will return as surely as the rising sun, so we need to make sure that effective programs and plans are in place.

These days we have all quickly become experts on the catastrophic increases in the prices of food and fuel. This is not an American issue but a global concern that in many countries is pushing starvation. Robert Zoellick, head of the World Bank, warns that the unfolding food crisis could force 100 million people deeper into destitution and set back efforts to reduce world poverty by seven years.[7] In countries like Indonesia this is especially unsettling, because for the poor family food costs are between 50 and 54 percent of its daily budget.[8] A similar situation exists for lower-income American families, though as yet without such severe consequences. Even before the current catastrophe combining fuel and food increases, the Census Bureau and United Stated Department of Agriculture (USDA) in 2006 estimated that 10.9 percent of American households were "food insecure"—and what kind of euphemism for "hungry" is that?—accounting for 35.5 million people.[9]

H. Eric Schockman, president of the Los Angeles–based MAZON: A Jewish Response to Hunger organization, captured this crisis well in remarks before the California State Assembly in May 2008, when he pointed out that the average American family spends 12 to 13 percent of its income on food (both inside and outside the home), but that at the poverty line a family *should* be spending 33.3 percent of its income on food to have "any chance of obtaining a minimally adequate diet."[10] He also cited the fact that for lower-income families the prices of food in the "thrifty food plan" jumped 5.6 percent in the one-year period between March 2007 and March 2008.[11] Of course, like the federal minimum wage, food support programs like Food Stamps are not indexed to inflation, so any increase goes right to the bottom line, and if there is no bottom line, past the fat and to the bone.

Fuel is the other stake in the heart of poor families, especially since transportation costs go along with holding down a job. This is a particularly difficult problem for rural families. A story in the *New York Times* included estimates that as much as 15 percent of some rural incomes were now being drained into the gas tanks of pickups used to get people to work.[12] The adjustments of urban families are as widely recognized and reported, but there are few stories of success in finding relief. The urban transportation system in the U.S. is not cheap, and infrastructure investment has not maintained the kind of pace that would provide the flexibility to expand to meet the increased demand caused by soaring gasoline prices. Few cities make it possible for lower-income and working families to simply make their way by foot or climb on a bicycle to travel the many miles to work. Other reactions, such as some districts changing the school schedule to four days a week to save fuel costs for buses, force families to pay more for childcare and after-school care when the parents are at work.

The other accelerating crisis around fuel pricing will impact fuel oil and heating costs across the board. The Low-Income Home Energy Assistance Program (LIHEAP) is not an entitlement program, but a "first-come, first-served" fund administered on the state level with heavy lobbying and involvement by state-based utility companies. Having a fixed allocation obviously means that fewer families will likely get assistance in helping with energy bills, just at a time when they need assistance the most. Even if the same number of families were to receive aid, the assistance would only nick the total bill, given the rate at which costs are increasing. Shutoffs are a real issue, as is the question of whether there will be sufficient funds in the dwindling LIHEAP pot to turn utilities back on. Reports estimate that millions of families with incomes less than $15,000 a year will experience a utility shutoff at some time during the year.[13] In colder and hotter parts of the country, shutoffs for lower-income and elderly people quite simply mean that people will die. The classic analysis of such a crisis, the Chicago heat wave in 1995, argues the case with more conviction than I could ever hope to,[14] though the response has still not been to move to create real solutions to this problem.

Responses to global warming are vitally important and gaining a national, if not a global, consensus more rapidly than alleviating the vise grip that food and energy inflation has on lower-income and working families. A number of the proposals are novel and innovative. It worries me, however, that the full impact of some of these pricing and taxing schemes on lower-income families' energy needs and minimal consumption requirements seems less central in the debate.

The last time such a squeeze began to push lower-income families against the wall, the response was an increase in the EITC payment levels. The quid pro quo for price increases driven by responses to global warming should be an increase in LIHEAP funding to more realistic amounts, and these amounts should perhaps be indexed to food and fuel prices. Bringing reality to the debate, we should not simply adjust EITC upward (though such increases are always appreciated), but we should change LIHEAP from a "good luck if you can get it program" to an equitable entitlement program that is then factored into every family's basic income allotments and entitlements. Speaking about entitlements is heresy in recent political debates, but if we are ever to make significant strides in building citizen wealth, it will not be on the basis of a wink-and-nod approach to lower-income and working families, but a real reach-out and push-up program that allows families to build wealth and keep the devil away from their door.

8

The Debt Trap

Can we really build wealth by using debt? Debt is hardly the same as savings or securities. Debt is something we have to pay someone else and, usually, very dearly. I could have a lively debate with you that debt reduces wealth, especially in the short run, rather than something that helps create wealth.

But we have also agreed that mortgages, which are obviously a form of debt, can help families build equity in their homes that can be converted to cash at some point or be used as collateral, thereby creating real citizen wealth. We have also realized that mortgage debt only becomes real ownership and wealth once the debt has been repaid, or the value of the property has risen higher than the balance remaining on the mortgage. When that does not happen, as we have also seen, then the mortgage holder forecloses and the family and the community suffer irreparably.

I think this conundrum is both difficult to resolve and a problem we will also have to embrace, because there is hardly a more constant companion for lower-income and working families than debt. Credit cards, payday loans, home loans, school loans—all combine to create a constant drumbeat of debt that promises in some cases the prospect of security and financial solvency, but also comes with huge risks that are often less than fully contemplated by the many policies and programs that embrace taking on debt as essential to creating citizen wealth.

Borrowing for Education

One of the largest puzzles centers on education-based debt. In many circles, we regard the purchase of higher education as a prerequisite to individual and class mobility, and as an opportunity to achieve citizen wealth, especially for lower-income and working young people. Without a doubt, all studies indicate that the higher the level of educational attainment the greater the likelihood of increased income (and in many cases wealth).[1]

Unfortunately, the price of higher education seems paved with debt, and until the credit crises of 2008, this debt was also increasingly being held by private lenders at variable rates reminiscent of the worst of the subprime offerings. In 2005/2006, according to a study done by the Institute for Higher Education Policy, federal educational loans were close to $69 billion, and private educational loans totaled $16 billion and were growing at a rate projected at 25 percent a year.[2] More disturbing to me is that the report nails the issue: "Not everyone receives perfect information about financial aid, and low-income students are among those most misinformed about the financial aid process overall. Thus targeted outreach to these students to ensure they are receiving comprehensive information about the pros and cons of private loan borrowing is critical."[3] The report also found that many students are not getting full value out of the federal Stafford loan program before resorting to private lenders, and in some cases they are not accessing federal loan support at all.

All this matters greatly. The federal educational loan program charges a lower interest rate and does not require a credit test, while private loans, when available, usually have variable rates, frequently with a teaser rate to attract the borrower and therefore a higher average rate. In addition to the problem of outreach and education for lower-income borrowers, there is something that feels predatory in this situation. Young people, desperate for the ticket to a brighter future that society claims higher education can punch, are forced to the private market to cover gaps in financing that colleges have created because of huge cost increases that are not covered by federal loan limits. The eager young student is pushed to the wall with the choice of taking a loan wherever she can find one or forgoing educational opportunities. The current credit crisis greets us with a barrage of articles in the daily papers detailing the desperation facing students trying to find resources, especially to attend local community and technical colleges where federal loans seem harder to access.[4]

Education may still be, next to housing, the best case for debt for lower-income families, because there may still be a payoff for them if they can wend their way through the maze of financing options. More commonly, though, debt is simply a burden. For lower-income families, too often this means credit cards, payday lending, pawnshops, check-cashing stores, and a host of other "financial services" that are roadblocks on the path to building, and keeping, citizen wealth.

Credit Card Debt

Credit cards have become ubiquitous. The last available figures, from 2001, indicate that more than 80 percent of white Americans have them, as well

Table 6 Percent of Credit Card–Indebted Families in Debt Hardship, 1992–2001

	1992	2001
African Americans		
Overall	9	13
Income Group		
$0–$14,999	31	31
$15,000–$29,999	7	13
$30,000–$49,999	4	14
$50,000 or more	3	3
Hispanics		
Overall	14	13
Income Group		
$0–$14,999	17	20
$15,000–$29,999	8	8
$30,000–$49,999	22	17
$50,000 or more	13	11
Whites		
Overall	11	14
Income Group		
$0–$14,999	19	28
$15,000–$29,999	13	21
$30,000–$49,999	11	16
$50,000 or more	6	6

Source: Demos calculations from the 1992 and 2001 Survey of Consumer Finances (income groups in 2002 dollars). Debt hardship is defined as a debt-to-income ratio greater than 40 percent.

as 59 percent of African Americans and 53 percent of Hispanics. All of these percentages represent increases over the previous ten years, many of them significant.[5] With credit comes debt, and 84 percent of African Americans were carrying balances on their cards, 75 percent of Hispanics, and 51 percent of white Americans.[6] The level of debt rose in the same period: up 20 percent for Hispanics to $3691, up 22 percent for African Americans to $2950, and up a whopping 41 percent for white families to $4281.[7] A study by Demos entitled "Costly Credit" recognized as well the frightening concept of "debt hardship," defined as debt sufficient to take up 40 percent of a household's income. The Demos figures shown in Table 6 are stunning.

The fact that families with less than $15,000 in income can obtain credit cards is probably a story in itself, but clearly lower-income— and other—families making less than $50,000 per year are using credit cards not to build and access wealth, but simply to survive when there is more month than money by using them to purchase basic necessities. In doing so, as the Demos chart shows starkly, they are also failing to survive very well, since larger and larger shares of their income are being used for plain and simple debt service. This is not a family business model that works.

The deregulation of credit cards has made that industry wildly lucrative in recent years. Between 1990 and 2004, credit card industry profits exploded rising from $6.4 billion to $30.2 billion per year.[8] Late fees and additional charges arising from purchases in excess of established credit limits totaled $14.8 billion in a classic example of how much money can be made from a business model based on "gotcha."[9] The credit card industry is rife with predatory-like practices, including unilateral increases in fees, interest rates, and additional assessments, sometimes based on triggers that the consumer neither understands or has any way to know exist, like slow payments to other lenders or credit score changes unrelated to the payment history with their credit card company. Credit card industry lobbying for more stringent rules blocking access to bankruptcy has also made many American families seem like modern examples of inmates of debtors prisons on work release.

Payday Lending

Without credit card access, though, the picture is hardly better, because in those situations families stretched to the breaking point are thrust into the arms of payday lenders and other financial operations with very high interest rates such as pawnshops. Fees here are estimated to cost such families close to $3.4 billion per year,[10] which converted to annualized interest rates would top 400 percent.[11] A study by ACORN Canada of the payday lending industry in that country found that a payday borrower was likely to be caught in the cycle of borrowing against his check more than ten times over a twelve-month period.[12] In the U.S. the Demos report cites the similarly alarming statistic that 90 percent of payday loans are to borrowers who take out five or more payday loans per year.[13]

Payday lending, as the name indicates, is a short-term loan against a check not yet received from an employer. Payday lenders, like our tax-prep friends with their RALs, are not able to finance this without the help of some of the largest financial institutions in the world. ACORN Canada's work on payday lending over the last four years found that the largest operator was Dollar Financial, which was of course owned by DFG Holdings, Inc., in the United States. The financiers behind the payday lending industry as unearthed by the ACORN Financial Justice Center included PNC Bank, JPMorgan Chase, Morgan Stanley, Bank of America, Wachovia, and Wells Fargo.[14] Having dealt with many of the top executives of these banks for years, I find it goes past irony sometimes to hear them tout their programs promoting "financial literary" or "financial education" when they are profiting by tens of millions from such financial inabilities in the cruelest of ways. Interestingly, ACORN Canada's efforts have led to legislation allowing individual provinces to regulate payday lending and apply caps on effective interest rates no greater than 35 percent,[15] and the industry, instead of going out of business, has proved sustainable and has continued to offer its services at these lower rates. Such legislation in various forms has now been passed in British Columbia and Ontario.[16] Similar legislation has also been passed in North Carolina, New Mexico, New Jersey, and several other states as the result of work by coalitions of ACORN, the well-regarded Center for Responsible Lending, and others.[17]

Microfinance

The promise of using debt to create citizen wealth is best realized in the highly regarded microcredit program devised in Bangladesh by Nobel Laureate Muhammad Yunus. Heralded by Yunus and his supporters as an effective antipoverty and wealth-building measure, these loans are often for very small amounts and focus on enabling individuals to begin small, informal enterprises while paying off the debt incrementally over time. Millions of such loans have reportedly now been made around the world. The United Nations, former President Bill Clinton, and many others have called microfinance an important innovation for lower-income families.

Exciting applications of social networks like Kiva have sprung up to match potential individual small lenders with small microenterprises and provide low-interest microloans to these families and their start-ups. The head of Kiva, Premal Shah, estimates that in coming years the network could provide loans totaling $36 million through such a matching program.[18]

Microfinance has taken small steps over the last thirty years seeking traction in the United States, beginning with the work undertaken in eastern Arkansas by the Winthrop Rockefeller Foundation in partner-ship with the Grameen Bank headed by Yunus. More recently, Ben Bernanke, the chairman of the Federal Reserve Bank, spoke to a meet-ing of Accion USA in San Antonio, which is perhaps the largest of the microcredit operations in the United States. He noted that since 1991, Accion USA had "loaned $180 million to nearly 20,000 borrow-ers in thirty-five states."[19] Bernanke drowned the movement with faint praise and a sharp point, however, noting that such loans work better in the "informal" economy where there are no problems with licenses, taxes, and other U.S. business requirements. He also noted that credit cards, home equity loans, credit lines from banks, and other financial services are perhaps more accessible than microfinance as financing instruments for small business. Interestingly, he did not mention Small Business Administration (SBA) loans, no doubt for good reason. He also did not say the obvious: that most microfinance is really more about simple survival rather than either sustainability or building busi-ness enterprises.

In the developed world, microfinance too often is a personally sub-sidized debt replacing a state obligation to assist in alleviating poverty at the most fundamental level. This is not to say that there are not success stories where outstanding and entrepreneurial individuals have parlayed just a few dollars into thriving businesses employing tens of people. These are exceptions, though, not the rule. It takes a horse to beat a horse, though, and as long as there is no other viable mass-based antipoverty mechanism, microfinance will be part of the game in our world. However, it is hard to believe that debt is an effective antidote to poverty or a pathway to even the most basic levels of citizen wealth.

The real issue that underlies all of these financial mechanisms, ei-ther laudatory or predatory, is the fact that low-income and working families, and many others from students to aspiring small business people, have credit needs that are not being responsibly met in the marketplace, especially for short-term credit at affordable rates. In another day, and in some other countries, credit unions have been an alternative, pooling family wealth to allow more affordable credit and a "community" that allows the building of trust and therefore credit to handle short-term needs at reasonable terms.

One of the vaunted initiatives of the antipoverty programs of the 1960s stressed the importance of building credit unions among the poor, yet the national policy and program for the last twenty to twenty-five years has been exactly the opposite, focusing more on consolidating credit unions to achieve scale and efficiency and making many of these credit unions resemble, well, banks, more than anything else. It was shocking to read that some large credit unions had significant losses from their exposure to subprime loans, just as large banks had experienced. All of this has been joined to resistance to chartering new credit unions, especially in lower-income communities. Admittedly, credit unions charging lower interest rates on short-term and consumer loans are not going to have the cushion to expand based on their narrow margins. However, with technological improvements on deposits, collections, and basic banking and standard Internet efficiencies, these institutions could have been an important player in building citizen wealth, and they have not risen to the challenge.

Similarly, the hope represented by cooperatives in European and Scandinavian countries, particularly in providing access to goods at lower prices and therefore in extending family income, is less an opportunity in contemporary America for regular families. We are all surprised to find that State Farm Insurance and Land O'Lakes are cooperatives. It all seems so out of touch and reminiscent of another time, so Minnesota or something—but not something we associate with where we live and work. Yet this kind of cooperative model, sometimes enmeshed in family or ethnic relationships, has frequently facilitated wealth creation in a powerful way.

Family and ethnic savings societies are often held responsible for the ability for Korean, Chinese, and other groups to enter the greengrocer market in many urban areas or start other small business ventures and restaurants through cooperative lending agreements. Burial societies begun by Jewish and other immigrant groups in New York and elsewhere over the years often functioned successfully as larger-scale, patient sources of capital behind their members' ventures into small business enterprises. Community saving schemes among the Vietnamese have frequently been credited for the successful entry of many into the fishing and shrimping industries on the Gulf Coast where boats alone often cost over $100,000.

We need to shift the paradigm again from a reliance on debt-based gimmicks that have become continually predatory to capital acquisition strategies that allow for the real development of citizen wealth. This should be our national policy and a central part of our program, rather than simply turning out our pockets to meet debt payments to huge financial institutions with precious few hopes of sustainability and only marginal chances at survival.

Immigrant Credit and Remittances

For immigrants there is unquestionably a lot of financial activity around credit cards, though it is hard to tell if this is a path to citizen wealth or simply the default system for immigrants, especially the undocumented. Bank of America, for example, began offering a card that did not require a social security number throughout the Los Angeles area in 2007 before a national rollout to customers. Customers simply had to have a Bank of America account and to have gone three months without an overdraft.[20] Interestingly, research into the unbanked is also finding that credit cards are common substitutes among younger, "ethnic" consumers,[21] which may also hint at a way that prepaid and stored-value cards are evolving up the credit chain into Visa, MasterCard, and similar products and bypassing banking for immigrant families completely.

Card usage also allows some facility for transferring remittances, which are payments made by immigrant workers to their families and others back home, making them especially popular along the border between the United States and Mexico. The cardholders can sometimes have duplicates and PIN numbers sent to relatives across the border to facilitate transfers or other card-to-card or card-to account transactions. International remittances generally have been one of the more shameful episodes of predatory pricing to captive markets, and a lot of work is happening in this area. The Transnational Institute for Grassroots Research and Action (TIGRA) coalition has been one response in recent years.[22] ACORN and ACORN Mexico have long worked with Citibank to try and smooth this problem along the Rio Grande border, especially since Banamex, one of the largest Mexican banks, is also owned by Citi, though it has been a much more intractable problem than many where we have made more progress. Similarly, HSBC also owns one of the largest banks in Mexico but has been slow to respond to us about either north–south issues or how immigrant-to-home-country transactions can be more effectively and fairly priced.

Competition generally has driven down the overall pricing structure of remittances from the Western Union–dominated heyday of the business (talk about a business model based on lower-income families!) as global transaction costs have also come down due to technology. In some countries like Kenya transfers using cellphones rather than credit cards have become ubiquitous, and such a system could spread globally, which would facilitate "loading" the cell with money via normal payment regimes and then transferring it via a long-distance call home.

The hard conclusion at this point, though, is that unfortunately outside of home mortgages and precious few other benefits, the picture is bleak for immigrants when it comes to citizen wealth. Despite our best intentions at defining the range and depth of citizen wealth, policy makers and politicians have hijacked the system quite thoroughly and have indeed virtually defined the notion of "citizen" wealth within the narrowest framework and meaning of citizens and citizenship, and within the most skinflint sense of wealth as well. Until we have a more open and democratic view of immigration and its value and a human rights and social justice perspective on immigrants themselves and their families, we will have to settle for being ashamed of ourselves and sentencing such families to not only being on the run, but to poverty as well, unless they are lucky enough by their own lights to escape both while here in America.

9

The "Maximum Eligible Participation" Solution

There may be a national consensus around the value of the Earned Income Tax Credit program that ensures its continuance, and perhaps even its expansion, but other programs wish they could find as much love. To build citizen wealth, we need to aggressively use *all* existing programs, no matter how many scars and warts they may have, because the passage of new initiatives is at the least years away. Many of these programs do not have the same level of support as EITC, which policy makers and politicians can defend as supporting hard-working families. Some, like the Food Stamp program, have supportive constituencies, but others were avowedly created to share the wealth of the nation with the poorest of its citizens and thereby provide some small share of family security.

There was a phrase from the 1960s that became a government mandate devised by Richard Boone calling for "maximum feasible participation" of the poor in a series of programs. Boone was not talking about benefits but empowerment.[1] I would like instead to talk about a modern adaptation of this slogan—"maximum eligible participation." We need a vision of maximum eligible participation and a campaign to achieve it as galvanizing as the movement for civic participation of the poor became in the old Office of Economic Opportunity (OEO). We need to create ways to ensure that all individuals and families eligible for any program or entitlement actually receive them. Such a situation would be empowering as well. As we can see in the current governmental bailout of the banking system, there is now no such concept as "breaking the bank," but we need to imagine a concerted effort by government, organizations, and individuals to enable eligible families to get access to the "bank" of benefits that is lawfully theirs.

Food Stamps

A look at the experience of the Food Stamp Program,[2] one of the few remaining entitlement programs, is instructive. The last major increase in participation was during President Lyndon B. Johnson's War on Poverty in the 1960s. Millions of new participants enrolled in the program because there was a change in outlook and outreach. Rather than dissuade applications, government policy encouraged eligible families to apply and even self-certify. It might be a stretch to say that the government was welcoming, but there was a period where the government was not overtly hostile to program applicants. Likewise, barriers to welfare programs and assistance also were lowered by several favorable Supreme Court decisions, and the programs were supported by a public and policy climate that saw reduction of poverty and creation of citizen wealth as a social, political, and economic good. The emergence of deeply rooted programs like VISTA (Volunteers in Service to America) volunteers and Community Action Partnerships (CAPs) facilitated massive outreach and effective assistance to help those applying for benefits.

The welfare rights movement also played a critical role in increasing access to benefits, both as part of the direct program of the organization and as an indirect result of the high profile and consistent action and advocacy of the organization. The National Welfare Rights Organization (NWRO), founded in 1966 by Dr. George Wiley following a march in Ohio to resist welfare benefit cutbacks, had quickly grown to become perhaps the largest organization of poor people of its time. Using an array of tactics drawn from the civil rights movement and from Wiley's own stint as deputy director of CORE (Congress of Racial Equality), the organization focused on two kinds of strategies in different places. One, advanced by Columbia University professors Richard Cloward and Frances Piven, was a "break the bank" strategy of trying to enroll all eligible welfare recipients in the program, thereby demonstrating need and leveraging pressure on the system through the fear of militancy and the specter of urban riots in order to force a significant increase in benefits to allow families to live adequately.[3] The other strategy, developed in the field by NWRO organizers, particularly by Bill Pastreich in the Massachusetts organization, concentrated on "minimum standard" campaigns, where underutilized benefits or language creating new entitlements existed in law or in rules and regulations directing welfare departments, but in practice were meted out on a discretionary basis. The campaigns were designed under an organizing theory of "equal protection" to find welfare recipients who had received the benefits and convert discretionary application into local and statewide entitlements for any recipient who was similarly qualified for benefits. In a short period in the late 1960s the Massachusetts organization was able to use direct action, demonstrations, and civil disobedience to expand allowances to furniture and household supplies as well as school, winter, and spring clothing for children.[4]

Whether in Massachusetts or other states, the high profile of NWRO and its activism certainly expanded the rolls of welfare recipients and participation in eligible benefits, especially in urban areas. The organization also generated excitement and the involvement of volunteers, including VISTA and CAP staffers who linked their individual work plans to the program of expanding benefits wherever they were in the country. Grievance systems and individual advocacy found a role in hundreds of cities even outside of the NWRO organizational influence. Cloward and Piven believed that the organization never embraced the enrollment campaign as a major organizational program, and indeed they were correct, yet there was a flood tide from its work that allowed many boats to rise, including the level of participation in government assistance programs. They were undoubtedly correct as well that NWRO was at least nominally a membership organization, and that both leadership and membership pressure were often more in the direction of improving benefits and reaching the elusive goal of adequate income than recruiting new members by walking "eligibles" onto the rolls.[5] The response to successful pursuit of the minimum standards approach in states like Massachusetts eventually became a "flat grant" system that raised benefits across the board for all welfare recipients, though it eliminated what had been an amazingly effective organization building and membership recruitment tool.

Importantly, there was a growing recognition by lower-income families that welfare, food stamps, and other programs should not continue to be stigmatized in a society that worshiped work, no matter what the individual story or circumstance. These program benefits were rights, just as NWRO asserted, because they were entitlements under law in the same way that voting or citizenship created rights— and therefore such entitlements should be embraced and used fully for their designed purposes. This did not necessarily reflect a universally popular consensus despite President Johnson's call to eliminate poverty, and there continued to be pushback against every advance. The legal regime and the public forum were never aligned, so the pendulum could, and would, move back against the poor whenever community-based organizations were less able to continue their organizing and advocacy.

As the shadow of the 1960s lengthened the idealism of the Johnson administration's Great Society dissipated in the tragedy of Vietnam. The energy and capacity of narrowly focused movements and rights-based campaigns for welfare recipients, tenants, and others shrank to the degree that there were no effective national or community responses to the clawback of benefits and participation that came later in the 1970s and 1980s. NWRO tried to oppose the national flat grant program embodied in Daniel Patrick Moynihan's Family Assistance Plan (FAP) under President Richard Nixon in order to use the last vestiges of the movement and the moment to win a higher standard of payments, closer to the adequate income program it had pursued as a core program under the banner of "$5500 or Fight" for a family of four on welfare. In hindsight, we can see now that NWRO did not recognize that the sun had set rather than simply going behind a cloud. The organization, in parallel with the conservative opposition, worked to prevent passage of the FAP, hoping that another and better program would take its place. Instead, welfare devolved over more than a twenty-five-year period into something that President Clinton would call "not welfare as we know it" and the even more limited system of entitlements that we know today.

Nonetheless, I would argue that the first step in asset building needs to be the achievement of full utilization of existing programs and policies that are already on the books, in the streets, authorized and funded, but that are not living up to their potential. This was a lesson from the 1960s that had huge value yet may be lost today in the sweep of nostalgia for long hair and tie-dye T-shirts.

A program like Food Stamps, which benefits both farmers and low-income families, is a perfect example of this dilemma because participation rates have been plummeting over the last twenty years. In creating citizen wealth we need to access all of these dollars that are being left somewhere on the table, in this case the dining table.

The Food Stamp program is not small and inconsequential. In March 2008 there were 27,878,875 people on food stamps, an increase of 1.5 million over the previous year.[6] And yet only two of every three of those eligible actually receive Food Stamp benefits.[7]

Programs for the Poor That Need Increased Participation

The amount of money, whether in Food Stamps or other programs, that goes unclaimed is huge, as the chart produced by Liz Wolff, ACORN research director, and reproduced here as Table 7, indicates.[8]

Full participation in Food Stamps alone would give an additional 12 million Americans another $14 billion in benefits. Perhaps as important, the USDA and private organizations like the Food Research and Action Center estimate that every dollar spent in a community in food stamps has double the economic impact in economic stimulus.[9] In short, the government and the benefited families would be doubling down on a huge opportunity at citizen wealth. Given food inflation the offset has another springboard effect, not even counting the other benefit of better health (and lower healthcare costs!) that comes from better and affordable nutrition. This kind of win-win-win-win situation is rare at the race track but unheard of for lower-income families.

The chart shows that there are also tremendous benefits if we could achieve maximum eligible participation with other federal programs, particularly, as I have argued about LIHEAP, if it were converted to an entitlement program. The Women and Infant Children (WIC) nutrition program has achieved significant results in offsetting infant mortality and supporting healthier birth-weight babies, but the gaps are obvious. The signups for the Medicaid SCHIP program have also lagged behind eligibility despite the significant benefits it offers.

The bottom line in benefits if there were full participation is breathtaking. The numbers are $38 billion for Food Stamps, $12 billion for SCHIP, and $5.1 billion for WIC, and we could throw another $1 billion into the pot if we could add LIHEAP. Achieving full participation in all of these programs, either separately or combined, would be a

Table 7 The Impact of Nonparticipation in Federal Antipoverty Programs

State	Eligible But Not in Medicaid and SCHIP	Missed in Medicaid and SCHIP Aid	Eligible but Not Using Food Stamps	Missed in Food Stamps Aid	Number Missing WIC, per Month*
Alabama	131,245	$173,185,486	247,799	$269,109,389	55,300
Alaska	26,702	$115,479,638	24,048	$36,179,518	10,991
Arizona	334,128	$510,890,852	280,144	$324,440,624	81,814
Arkansas	118,516	$146,963,041	150,137	$161,643,715	37,552
California	1,815,342	$1,760,746,478	1,384,587	$1,644,058,347	597,600
Colorado	209,686	$389,592,327	164,138	$209,610,894	39,285
Connecticut	88,925	$201,778,100	94,064	$106,939,437	22,896
Delaware	30,912	$70,160,835	29,658	$31,678,661	8,786
District of Columbia	16,289	$54,953,183	23,812	$27,813,954	6,572
Florida	995,625	$1,652,640,271	742,436	$882,014,063	184,155
Georgia	424,869	$907,229,163	410,556	$476,261,280	122,991
Hawaii	27,780	$53,896,439	35,589	$59,833,004	14,098
Idaho	60,748	$127,137,727	56,515	$62,134,742	16,628
Illinois	444,025	$791,353,120	497,392	$610,299,377	121,480
Indiana	211,765	$410,213,737	252,633	$284,909,658	60,606
Iowa	61,830	$125,629,247	122,003	$132,011,771	30,235
Kansas	71,965	$133,171,416	105,578	$108,601,805	29,056
Kentucky	138,638	$363,958,677	214,677	$235,174,669	55,799
Louisiana	201,137	$387,466,938	242,516	$301,466,268	56,708
Maine	31,090	$132,900,698	45,661	$48,223,450	10,797
Maryland	187,936	$433,086,244	162,647	$178,996,131	54,518
Massachusetts	151,110	$411,255,343	241,107	$235,542,488	51,631
Michigan	234,719	$401,214,755	436,505	$476,925,013	100,040
Minnesota	114,363	$274,860,706	165,668	$177,231,676	58,371
Mississippi	148,949	$252,146,109	242,381	$274,539,554	44,158
Missouri	181,879	$327,056,879	186,860	$173,645,017	58,225
Montana	42,243	$101,742,348	42,464	$46,828,858	8,309
Nebraska	49,207	$104,242,984	65,978	$68,532,199	18,318
Nevada	132,097	$190,867,437	82,216	$86,682,361	23,093
New Hampshire	32,082	$83,868,628	34,763	$35,712,602	7,549
New Jersey	334,235	$728,380,377	252,029	$283,199,665	65,219
New Mexico	116,671	$256,850,509	110,670	$114,596,286	27,950
New York	580,112	$1,630,802,712	837,794	$1,050,794,439	208,646
North Carolina	376,073	$868,355,506	456,001	$491,550,355	104,993
North Dakota	18,487	$35,640,488	24,333	$26,416,344	6,200
Ohio	294,183	$636,883,651	500,583	$595,773,363	121,252
Oklahoma	162,326	$272,014,239	170,532	$182,987,809	51,920
Oregon	150,575	$279,829,140	158,471	$169,075,717	45,315
Pennsylvania	296,426	$646,802,341	504,754	$546,345,543	105,080
Rhode Island	24,869	$69,432,453	41,311	$45,676,457	10,603
South Carolina	174,658	$270,578,258	210,489	$232,203,348	50,296
South Dakota	23,677	$52,742,960	32,869	$37,190,627	9,461
Tennessee	188,730	$373,969,572	249,024	$279,225,415	69,076
Texas	1,669,733	$3,116,398,696	1,266,083	$1,419,025,360	390,790
Utah	123,368	$200,679,379	75,496	$80,457,964	27,913
Vermont	16,079	$35,401,417	23,916	$25,381,333	6,992
Virginia	259,888	$482,068,250	244,758	$253,970,198	61,457
Washington	195,700	$317,401,445	249,052	$276,387,587	72,049
West Virginia	62,732	$115,289,267	99,111	$98,655,320	20,749
Wisconsin	126,915	$200,515,252	204,058	$192,271,654	50,531
Wyoming	17,935	$42,526,324	13,983	$15,178,435	5,354
Total for All States	11,929,179	$21,722,251,044	12,509,844	$14,183,403,745	3,499,405

* Federal Special Supplemental Nutrition Program for Women, Infants, and Children. Source: Liz Wolff, ACORN Research Report, January 2008.

Table 7 Continued

Annual WIC Amount Lost	Eligible Households Not Getting LIHEAP	LIHEAP Aid Amount Lost	Eligible Children Not Getting Childcare Subsidies	Possible Additional Childcare Dollars	Total Amount Missed
$30,246,970	272,582	$39,693,330	162,600	$542,684,778	$1,055,192,535
$6,106,488	33,650	$19,742,283	28,200	$175,720,266	$353,228,194
$33,331,178	363,435	$69,549,099	185,400	$675,531,546	$1,613,743,299
$15,541,980	168,397	$21,228,990	61,800	$103,423,140	$448,800,867
$262,609,261	3,415,720	$764,475,497	844,200	$4,947,708,900	$9,379,598,483
$14,882,654	263,168	$78,276,561	114,600	$429,667,050	$1,122,029,485
$11,608,160	323,361	$128,815,061	57,600	$694,900,398	$1,144,041,157
$3,261,082	47,738	$13,529,314	41,400	$221,781,942	$340,411,834
$3,119,713	44,328	$15,275,506	22,800	$204,179,778	$305,342,134
$88,372,417	1,306,475	$236,970,767	697,800	$2,334,007,620	$5,194,005,138
$54,991,816	534,612	$103,548,313	363,600	$868,539,162	$2,410,569,735
$8,962,932	79,744	$19,922,795	53,400	$189,766,968	$332,382,138
$5,968,003	61,428	$15,609,596	63,600	$171,072,300	$381,922,368
$58,310,477	626,267	$226,320,298	504,000	$1,965,352,710	$3,651,635,981
$23,723,750	127,657	$27,875,671	193,200	$585,138,348	$1,331,861,164
$11,943,872	114,609	$34,258,396	107,400	$292,997,700	$596,840,987
$11,251,463	114,655	$40,357,316	112,800	$483,526,254	$776,908,255
$26,174,171	68,484	$7,824,396	151,200	$615,810,252	$1,248,942,166
$28,083,842	457,573	$162,178,737	310,800	$338,710,548	$1,217,906,333
$4,031,983	74,585	$32,819,473	31,800	$154,869,492	$372,845,096
$22,001,450	198,299	$67,775,689	123,000	$832,164,990	$1,534,024,504
$21,783,953	518,259	$271,180,918	209,400	$1,489,144,068	$2,428,906,769
$42,160,828	75,321	$16,675,975	475,800	$1,215,696,240	$2,152,672,811
$24,452,867	221,742	$83,677,528	153,000	$623,458,332	$1,183,681,108
$20,024,570	304,405	$53,772,776	199,800	$336,151,812	$936,634,821
$21,359,420	74,938	$17,464,771	217,800	$886,500,534	$1,426,026,622
$3,360,289	70,781	$27,553,600	31,200	$75,198,552	$254,683,647
$7,730,929	2,901	$717,368	80,400	$296,363,856	$477,587,335
$8,047,351	103,878	$51,939,000	27,600	$95,573,952	$433,110,101
$2,848,861	98,477	$39,191,893	42,600	$151,104,798	$312,726,782
$29,653,757	428,814	$161,559,938	224,400	$1,261,210,356	$2,464,004,093
$11,534,406	133,262	$16,646,084	138,600	$375,850,536	$775,477,821
$112,143,224	1,528,305	$520,189,191	765,600	$3,911,328,420	$7,225,257,986
$46,994,719	239,255	$35,250,552	625,800	$1,795,825,530	$3,237,976,662
$2,992,243	58,294	$23,731,429	22,200	$50,167,200	$138,947,703
$49,412,721	373,622	$59,893,944	279,600	$1,619,835,582	$2,961,799,262
$21,008,876	104,265	$10,803,270	118,200	$726,137,232	$1,212,951,427
$18,765,719	305,706	$79,903,922	127,800	$401,194,026	$948,768,524
$42,355,630	171,042	$38,794,949	435,600	$1,821,381,546	$3,095,680,010
$4,945,435	113,037	$40,902,155	31,200	$228,943,854	$389,900,354
$24,353,231	299,314	$59,499,422	117,000	$449,010,576	$1,035,644,835
$3,689,903	50,726	$26,395,653	28,200	$50,647,188	$170,666,331
$34,979,899	411,262	$136,795,446	259,200	$1,127,746,122	$1,952,716,454
$142,278,987	1,274,586	$419,516,760	740,400	$2,234,003,310	$7,331,223,113
$8,601,676	64,249	$16,659,891	66,600	$232,060,728	$538,459,637
$3,622,032	5,773	$2,767,549	36,600	$181,251,918	$248,424,249
$25,929,891	213,351	$44,815,232	175,800	$362,058,642	$1,168,842,213
$34,574,706	220,839	$88,743,724	323,400	$1,616,121,930	$2,333,229,393
$8,719,652	93,287	$19,586,259	60,000	$210,387,066	$452,637,565
$20,962,288	141,696	$51,128,191	172,200	$1,007,230,692	$1,472,108,078
$1,775,292	29,029	$10,145,043	27,600	$57,048,366	$126,673,461
$1,525,587,020	16,427,183	$4,551,949,520	10,444,800	$41,716,187,106	$83,699,651,017

huge step forward on the road to citizen wealth for lower-income families.

We may not have enough soldiers to suit up for a 21st-century war on poverty,[10] and forty years after Cloward and Piven's exciting call to arms most of the banks are bleeding if not broken, so the metaphor is not as lively, but it is hard to believe that we cannot assemble the troops to mount a campaign for maximum eligible participation that harvests the opportunities and dollars already available if we could achieve full utilization of existing programs.

This $83 billion (for all programs combined) is enough to make it worth waging at least a small war for citizen wealth, and worth engaging in some hand-to-hand contact in the neighborhoods and barrios of America.

TANF, Unemployment Insurance, and Childcare Credits

If all that is not enough, there are a couple of other big issues around benefits. One goes to the issue of making work pay, and the other, on the opposite side of the fence, seeks to make not working pay as well. The first involves unemployment insurance (UI), and the second involves TANF (Temporary Assistance to Needy Families).

Unemployment insurance is a huge headscratcher. This is real insurance, not welfare, paid for by workers to provide some level of benefit payments when they lose their jobs. It seems that roadblocks to actually getting unemployment benefits have been added by different states with the intention of scaring off eligible applicants despite the fact that they paid for these benefits personally. Much of the pushback has been led by employers at the state level fighting against their "experience rating," which goes up as more workers actually qualify for and receive benefits. There are waiting periods that can be time consuming. Automatic employer appeals are used by some firms as a delay tactic. In 2004, for example, $35.6 billion in benefits were paid to 2.56 million unemployed workers.[11] The federal government steps in only to help pay for "extended benefit" weeks in times of serious national unemployment. Here is the kicker, though. Looking at 2004 again, the Urban Institute, hardly an AFL-CIO front group, noted that only 31 percent of eligible unemployed received benefits in any typical week.[12] The problem lies squarely with the states, and that is where it will have to be forcefully engaged: "Between 1994 and 2003, UI receipt averaged less than 25 percent in 13 states and exceeded 45 percent in 7. This variation is linked to differences in both state UI policies and administrative activities."[13] There should be no mistake: "administrative activities" is a euphemism with a suit on, hiding a more plainspoken statement that in those states there were deliberate and often aggressive efforts made by state workers in unemployment offices to *keep* eligible workers from receiving the benefits that they had personally paid for. We have to stop this.

TANF is welfare-lite in the new, post-Clinton welfare regime, different from what we had ever known. The problem for many people is not getting on TANF but staying on, since the whole direction of the program is now designed to push recipients into work at whatever wage and situation as soon as possible. Problematically, the math (much like the old welfare math) still creates incentives to *stay* on TANF for many mothers with children, rather than to jump into a minimum-wage job while being careful not to lose critical benefits. The full package of benefits *with* TANF could in fact be a step toward income security, if not citizen wealth itself—but once again too few are collecting the full amount of supports.

One essential benefit that frequently supports TANF-approved work is a childcare subsidy, but many low-wage workers and their families do not realize that they are eligible for these childcare subsidies as well as TANF. In 2005 state income criteria ranged from 111 percent to 287 percent of the federal poverty level for a family of three ($16,090/year).[14] Unfortunately, this essential benefit is only an entitlement in a handful of states, and in fact twenty states had long waiting lists of qualified families and have in fact stopped even bothering to take new applications. First come, first served is not a plan for citizen wealth but a prescription for disaster. Reviewing the patchwork quilt of overlapping and contradictory information and standards among the states would lead most people to think that the government was playing "hide and seek" with a benefit program rather than accepting the reality that for families childcare support means everything in the ability to get work and hold on to to it.

Putting Together a National Participation Campaign

We need a national crusade to achieve maximum eligible participation, and it can be done. I think there are three critical pieces that make such a crusade possible now in a way we might not have imagined in the past.

First, we need to upgrade the technology of accessing benefits. The state and federal governments need to make the investment that allows online application systems, monitoring, and delivery of benefits. There are already important steps being taken by early adopters in several states for specific programs, and these experiments have taught valuable lessons. EITC is already accessible online. The bugaboos preventing some adaptation of technology are largely in the area of fraud prevention, but in every other way technology has increasingly addressed these concerns down to the point where one could "see" the applicant through a video calling system from an "application" computer to the "department" screen. There are many methods of testing and counterchecking identity. Scanning applications allow electronic transmission and retention of documents in a way vastly superior to file folders and kitchen cupboards. Electronic movement of money needs to meet the challenge of ending the problem of the "unbanked" among new Americans and lower-income and working families. I will talk about all of this more later, but this change is inevitable, so there is no reason not to accelerate progress now so that families can be well on their way to citizen wealth all the sooner.

Second, we need to make access and applications ubiquitous for eligible families *everywhere* they intersect any public authority: schools, government offices of all shapes and sizes, public libraries, community centers, Head Start centers, churches and other religious centers, nonprofits, recreation facilities—anywhere we can find the traffic and convince the landlord, whether private, public, or somewhere in between. The huge breakthrough in "motor voter" registration meant that when people showed up to get or renew a driver's license they were registered to vote as well. The program to use welfare offices to register voters was never really implemented but had the same promise.[15] Simple training either in-person by program representatives or through "webinars" would enable anyone anywhere to know enough to ask the question of potential eligibles and send them to the nearest computer station (and these need to be ubiquitous, as we have argued) and set them in motion to apply.

These first two steps get the low-hanging fruit where we can leverage public intersection of services, and it might touch some of the folks out there in the nooks and crannies who cannot be easily found in other ways (until there is an automatic and universal application system), but the heart of the third step that has to be taken is a plain and simple shoes-on-the-pavement, fists-to-the-doors outreach. The government needs to spend some money and make this happen. It is instructive to look at the dollars the Treasury Department under President George W. Bush began to invest when it had to do with preventing foreclosures and not only allowing the protection of home purchasers, but also allowing private and quasi-public financial institutions to survive. For the 3 million to 4 million homeowners facing foreclosure we have invested millions of dollars in outreach utilizing phone centers, door-to-door work, and anything that works to bring families *into* the system to see if their loans can be modified. Looking at the millions of eligible families, we need a similar investment in creating and preserving citizen wealth that sends the troops out beating the bushes to get everyone *into* this system where they can exercise their rights to benefits. These troops could be church groups, community organizations, AmeriCorps and VISTA volunteers, Teach-for America people, student volunteers, and, you got it, anyone and everyone.

This can and should be done, because it is right, would make a huge difference, and is a victory at our fingertips waiting to be grasped if we are willing to take hold of it.

Part III

Changing the Terms
of the Debate

10

Working with Corporations to Create an Asset Climate

I have touched on the ways that government, unions, community-based organizations, and even individuals can play an increasing role in creating citizen wealth, but if their efforts are to succeed we have to believe that corporations, especially those whose business model is most intricately entwined with the fortunes of lower-income and working families, can also be moved to see that it is in their interest to embrace citizen wealth strategies. Regardless of Bob Dylan's famous line that "you don't need a weatherman to know which way the wind blows,"[1] sometimes things move slowly, and it takes quite a lot of effort before big institutions begin to understand that the tide is turning and change is inevitable.

The question for all of us who are committed to increasing citizen wealth as a society is whether or not change can come and whether or not we are starting to see the wheels of progress slowly begin to turn. I may be cockeyed, but I believe there are some signs that justify optimism, and one of the first of these came from one of the most unlikely of places: our old friend, and foe, HSBC.

HSBC Turns the Tide
HSBC is not a household word in the United States, even though the bank has global stature and ranks among the top five largest financial institutions in the world with $152 billion in gross revenue in 2007 (after Citigroup, Crédit Agricole, Fortis, and Bank of America).[2] It

began life as the Hong Kong and Shanghai Banking Corporation in 1865 to finance trade between China and Europe. HSBC was a vital part of the British concession when Britain still called the shots in Hong Kong until the beginning of the twentieth century; the bank still has a mammoth building there and has its name firmly printed on all Hong Kong currency. HSBC's footprint is not as significant in North America, however, and its purchase of Household Finance seemed like a major initiative to expand in the U.S.

In the ACORN campaign to reform predatory practices by tax pre-parers, particularly on refund anticipation loans, we were continually thwarted every time our negotiating committee raised the issue of eliminating other fees besides the ones that the preparers themselves agreed to drop. HSBC was the largest and most aggressive of the lend-ers that supported RALs, with JPMorgan Chase and Santa Barbara Bank next in line. In the same way that we had needed H&R Block to take the lead in reducing fees and setting the pattern, we needed to stop playing "who's on first, who's on second" while shuttling back and forth between the preparers and the banks, and get additional fees taken off the RALs, especially since we could not eliminate them from the market.

We tried endlessly to get a seat at the table with HSBC to raise this issue and finally get to the bottom of the problem. Finally, with the help of Lisa Sodeika of the HSBC communications staff, Jordan Ash and I meandered through the office parks of New Jersey in late May 2007 with Pedro Rivas, one of ACORN's national leaders, to meet in HSBC's nondescript offices off the Interstate in Bridgewater. We were scheduled to visit with Stuart Tait, the managing director of HSBC's Taxpayer Financial Services division, which meant that he was the banker behind Block's RALs. We knew there had been pullback from some of the more onerous RAL practices. HSBC had released an advisory in March that it would not finance pretax-season RALs on the basis of W-2s,[3] which were among the nastiest loans in the RAL lineup, but even so we had no special reasons to be optimistic about the outcome of our meeting. In the same advisory the company had in fact maintained its commitment to financing the product for both H&R Block and Jackson Hewitt. This was just one of those meetings we were squeezing in between a meeting to continue to push Jackson Hewitt and another later that day with representatives of H&R Block.

Our hope was to continue to paint the parties into a tighter and tighter corner and hope something came from that.

Stuart Tait was of a different breed, though, and not simply because he had the British accent that came with the company's home country. We made our case about why we thought RALs were predatory. We also got right to the bottom line. We had been back and forth with H&R Block and Jackson Hewitt about eliminating the charges they said that HSBC was adding as additional fees to the RALs. I related the history of how we had gotten Block to eliminate its fees and explained that the reduction had made an enormous difference to customers. I said that I understood from them that they had tried to convince HSBC to drop its fee from the loans as well, but they had reported to me at the negotiating table that HSBC had pretty much told them to buzz off. I told Tait that if RALs were going to exist, we really needed to reduce the costs to make them less predatory, and though reducing fees would squeeze their pocket a little, it needed to be done.

Tait said he was new to this piece of the bank's business and was trying to get on top of all of the moving parts, but that frankly, for HSBC's part, he did not know about these fees and would have to get back to us on that. That was a surprise, but perhaps even more important, he said that he was reviewing everything about RAL financing and HSBC's role as a leading RAL lender and was preparing to make a recommendation to London in the coming months. When pushed by us a little further, he offered an additional and important insight by telling us that he was questioning whether any amount of money made this way had any value compared to the "damage it might do to the brand." We left the meeting on cloud nine. Tait seemed to understand the problem intuitively, and we could not believe that any analysis, much less the kind of due diligence he seemed to be bringing to the task, could not help but find that the harm done to the brand by RALs was huge. We could smell victory here.

Six months later in a huge conference room in the suburban Chicago office of HSBC, I, Mike Shea, head of ACORN Housing, and others sat around a larger conference table meeting the head of HSBC's U.S. operations and other top executives. This was a "relationship" meeting of sorts in the evolution of what had become our "partnership." After the pleasantries and once the big boss left the meeting, Tait passed on more news to us on RALs. The bottom line quickly became apparent. No matter how you dressed it up, HSBC had clearly decided not just to pull back, but to pull out of the RAL financing business altogether. The bank would fulfill its contracts with H&R Block and Jackson Hewitt, which had another year or so to run, but other than one other contract HSBC would unwind the rest of its RAL business. Damn the money, Tait had obviously concluded: Protect the company and the brand!

And the fees? Tait claimed that HSBC was not taking them. He also indicated that his staffers had pulled open the hood and changed the software in five or six places to prevent anyone else from adding fees to the product. It was hard not to believe him, and we were excited by this step forward. Had they really never been charging that fee? It is hard to tell still. There was definitely a fee, and it was going somewhere. We had nothing to gain by finding the end of the chain once all was said and done. The important thing to ACORN's Financial Justice Campaign was saving another $250 million for desperate low-income and working taxpayers who were grabbing the RALs and paying whatever they had to in order to get the money immediately.

JPMorgan Chase, FDI, and IRS Get in the Game

Later representatives from JPMorgan Chase told us in a teleconference that they were also willing to drop their fees on the RALs. They admitted that they charged such a fee, but they wanted to wait until the 2009 tax season to drop it (presumably so they could take one more whack at their customers in 2008). They knew they had to respond to HSBC's move in the marketplace and were bitter in discussing HSBC's new position. They had seen HSBC as a "fierce competitor" and the "most aggressive in the marketplace" in this area in trying to hold the lion's share of the RAL financing business, but for all that they were clearly less than excited at having to move to where the RALs were headed, and that was cheaper, much cheaper. They shared with us a fascinating PowerPoint deck that gave the history of the RAL product and showed how in 2008 it would be cheaper than they had ever imagined. H&R Block and HSBC were preparing to offer RALs with an effective interest rate of about 36 percent, and JPMorgan Chase intended to match that.

Never willing to let an opportunity slip, we continued to press them to "meet the market" and eliminate their fee now rather than a year later. We felt the tide was turning, and whether the cause was fear of a negative brand impact or a move to repentance and redemption, there was change in the air.

The FDIC under Sheila Bair, its director, was proving surprisingly nimble in beginning to address these questions under its regulatory charter. The FDIC had asked lenders to freeze the terms on adjustable rate mortgages (ARMs) in late 2007. Earlier the FDIC had also sent out an advisory giving extra credit under CRA for banks who were stepping up and making short-term loans to consumers more accessible and affordable and thereby potentially serving as an alternative to payday lending and other predatory practices. It was too early for a party, but not too early to wonder if RALs were headed for the dustbin of history.

Finally the Chase executive said in some exasperation, "What do you want? Do you want us to just abandon this business? And then what?"

I answered, "That's inevitable. Perhaps you should consider if you want to be the last big bank in this nasty business."

He had a point, though. If the big boys left the field, would the other institutions that came in to replace them be worse? He believed that would be the case. Obviously time will tell, but it hardly works as a business model to engage in an enterprise because others might make the money by doing even worse than you would.

In a recent postscript, the IRS announced during the heart of the 2008 tax season that the agency was also beginning to turn up its nose at RALs.[4] The IRS wrapped its concerns around the edges of the issue, initially noting that it had some concerns about disclosures and marketing, but that it was also mindful that tax preparers offering RALs had incentives to "inflate" the level of the possible refund to capture more of the high-dollar loan. Furthermore, by asking the question whether there was "inappropriate" use by tax preparers, the IRS seemed to be using a euphemism for "predatory." I am not going to quibble about the details, however, but rather I will hold my breath in the hope that the IRS will finally make the right rules.

The real point finally is Sheila Bair's and the one we have made repeatedly, that in building citizen wealth we have to have short-term lending options for lower-income and working families that are accessible and affordable—not payday lending joints, pawnshops, brothers-in-law, next-door neighbors, and RALs. If the tide is moving toward citizen wealth, surely it must be possible for institutions to find a way to make money well by doing the right thing.

11

Business Models That Embrace Citizen Wealth

I am probably not the first person many would think to call for the best quotes on how it might be possible for corporations to see as part of their mission *creating* more citizen wealth as opposed to *extracting* more wealth from citizens. I am unable to resolve the immediate contradiction, particularly given the massive evidence of exploitation in the financial system that is stripping so much wealth from families during this recession. But, contrary to all of that evidence, I believe I can argue that some businesses are so dependent on the low- and moderate-income market that this is a constructive tension built on the these firms' interests in their customers having more income and wealth, if for no other reason than to spend more money or invest more with them.

Surprisingly, I believe that we came the closest to seeing a real synchronization of interests around citizen wealth and asset building for lower- and moderate-income families with our old friends at H&R Block, even though Block has not been deluged with much fan mail in these pages thus far. There are other examples where major enterprises should see embracing citizen wealth as fundamental to their business model. AARP is an interesting case on the insurance and nonprofit side. Wal-Mart is a company that has frequently gone out of its way to earn our contempt and has become a symbol of blind disregard for much other than its bottom line—yet it could be both different and better because it depends on its lower-income and working-family customer base. Firms should also recognize the niche of developing competitive—and constructive—financial products as potential benefits for low- and moderate-income families, contributors to real citizen wealth, and market segments for their own investment and growth. Stored value card operations are good examples of products finding a market and growing robustly.

H&R Block Doing Right

After settling in 2004 with H&R Block, I heard regularly from Murray Walton. His business card said that he was an H&R Block vice president and compliance officer, but his duties also clearly included serving as the "relationships manager" with ACORN,[1] overseeing the three cities where we had pilot projects as part of the agreement and generally handling traffic and policing all parts of our agreement. When we had a problem, he tried to be a fixer within the limits of his authority within a large corporation. In return, he lobbied us on everything under the sun and generally was a character. His partner, Bernie Wilson, from the first days of our relationship proved to be quite a different guy and an evangelist and operator of another sort. When Murray moved on, claiming to be relocating to live in Ann Landers's old penthouse in Chicago,[2] a story I was never able to confirm or deny, Bernie became the guy on the other end of the partnership that we were forging out of the conflict of 2003–2004 between ACORN and H&R Block.

On that same spring day in late May 2007 somewhere between Newark and Paterson, Jordan Ash, director of ACORN's Financial Justice Center at the time, and I were supposed to meet Bernie for a cup of coffee and sketch out a plan for beginning negotiations on renewal of our three-year agreement. We were going to meet at a popular diner along some industrial canal in the warehouse district, but for more peace and quiet ended up walking over to a nearby hotel lobby, pushing some chairs together, and sitting down to talk and see where we were going.

One of the interesting things we had discovered in the course of our pilot program with the Marguerite Casey Foundation and our campaigns taking on H&R Block, Jackson Hewitt, and Liberty Tax Services was the importance for our own community organizations and members of making tax services truly accessible in lower-income neighborhoods. Since our first experiments in 2003 in Miami, New Orleans, and San Antonio, what we now called the ACORN Centers (originally the ACORN Tax Centers, then the ACORN Tax and Benefit Centers, and now this name, but I will get there) had done nothing but grow. In tax preparation, Ron Smith, our partnership manager with the IRS, informed us that by 2007, we had already become the third-largest nonprofit preparer in the country, trailing only AARP and the United Service Organization (on military bases). In 2008 we prepared tax returns for more than 50,000 families, providing more than $55 million worth of benefits.

The ACORN Centers had proven popular not only with the Marguerite Casey Foundation; the Citi Foundation, as part of that partnership, rated the half-million dollars a year it gave in support to the centers as the most productive grant it had ever given. With H&R Block, though, the existence of the ACORN Centers was always something of an issue. Although the partnership money was intended to do outreach for the EITC program, we had always agreed that we would not use Block's money to help build competition, and in some way H&R Block couldn't help but see the ACORN Centers as competition.

For a company like Block, which reports $60 billion worth of taxes annually on 20 million returns, we were in our view at best a pimple on an elephant's butt. Nonetheless, Jordan had reported to me that several times in recent years, Bernie had raised, first jokingly and then more seriously, that we allow Block to essentially "buy out" the ACORN Centers and have us simply refer our people to the nearest Block tax office. Who knows what he had in mind, but in fact we had become even more committed to the ACORN Centers as we saw their potential. In 2007, for example, we introduced benefit screening to allow our staff or volunteers to check on the computer to see if someone might be eligible for other benefits besides EITC while they were in the ACORN Center and had their tax information, income figures, and family size on the screen. We had great ambitions for this program if we could figure out how to make it work.

At our meeting in New Jersey, I laid out our basic interest in renewal and expansion of our partnership with Block, increasing the money, adding more pilots, and achieving higher outcomes—but nothing fancy or special, just essentially the same agreement on steroids. Bernie cleared his throat and started talking about the ACORN Centers, and

I cringed a little, believing that I was about to hear the pitch from Bernie that Jordan had warned me was going to come someday—that the centers were an issue and an obstacle to the growth of the partnership. Somehow his sentence started with the centers, but once I started really listening, it became apparent that the conversation was taking a different and unexpected direction.

Bernie was actually not talking about putting the ACORN Centers out of business, but about embracing and building them. In fact, I hoped I was piecing together the words correctly, because none of it was direct and all of it was tentative in the way ground-rules discussions can sometimes be, because Bernie seemed to be talking not about simply extending the agreement but about a real partnership in something much bigger. Bernie seemed to have taken a page out of our hymnal and was singing for all he was worth. Somehow in that hotel lobby the "new" Bernie version of H&R Block had become not the "show us and we'll make it better" H&R Block, but H&R Block as the anti-predator. He was talking about H&R Block as if a new business model were possible.

From the first time we negotiated with H&R Block it was clear that we were disturbing because our core constituency, working families with low and moderate incomes, was also the sweet spot in Block's existing business model. Then we had represented a threat because we could make inroads into the heart of Block's business and potentially hurt the company and, as we in fact found, impact its all-important brand. As we came to understand Block better we also learned that an important feature of its business model was mining its clientele, who came back year after year, because a large percentage of Block's business was with customers who were "preparer dependent" no matter how much the IRS might simplify the forms.

Our research showed that Block spent a lot of time and money in recent years trying to see if it could expand its business model by "up-selling" to the higher end of its client base among middle- and upper-middle-income clients. The argument for this part of the business model had been that if these folks were also preparer dependent they might see H&R Block as a brand and its offices and staff as "trusted advisors" and look to Block for advice on other financial services and even investments. Wall Street and the market had never been convinced, and so far the results were not changing their minds or increasing the value of the company's stock, so though the jury was still out the verdict seemed increasingly clear.

Similarly, H&R Block had spent time and money getting a bank charter to brand a separate Block Bank. We had met its CEO in Kansas City even before the charter was approved, and since Block had agreed to voluntarily abide by CRA guidelines nationally wherever it operated, we had not opposed the bank's formation.[3] We had not studied the bank in any detail, though, and it was hardly a blip on our radar. However, the company clearly felt that its new bank was going to be an important development in its future. We just did not think it concerned us.

On the other hand, Option One, Block's subprime lending operation based in Orange County, California, gave us nothing but heartburn. From the first time we sat down with H&R Block representatives we had agreed that this was an issue for us but that we would handle that problem separately if we could resolve our problem with Block's tax practices. Unfortunately, Option One had proven resistant to even meeting with us, and one excuse from Murray followed another until he would essentially concede that they were flipping him off even within the company despite Block's ownership position. It took years for us to get that meeting, and not long after that Option One began its quick slide over the edge into the subprime abyss along with the rest of its ilk.

Putting together all we knew, we were intrigued by Bernie's tentative inquiry into our interest in going a different direction. We agreed to a briefing later, and over several calls and meetings the new direction became clearer and something very different began to emerge that pulled the pieces together for us as well. It seemed to us that Block had decided not simply to embrace ACORN Centers but to look at embracing citizen wealth itself and, instead of chasing the high end of its market, to hunker down, just as we were doing, with its base of largely working-income clients and see if the company could grow by helping its clients grow their incomes and wealth. Block shared surveys and data with us that indicated that a huge percentage of its customers were eligible for other benefits, like food stamps and SCHIP, but were not getting them. Just as we had moved into benefits, Block also had done some pilot programs that tried to encourage eligibles by at least passing out applications for food stamps.

In two other areas where we faced problems, Block and Bernie seemed to have arrived at some things that looked like solutions. One was in the area of benefits, and the other was in banking.

The problem with our benefit platform was that it was cheap, like we were, and clunky, which was more of a problem. Once we had someone with us in the ACORN Center we had to take the income and family data and download it, then upload a separate program, and then run the benefit screen. What we wanted to be almost instantaneous took seemingly forever. To hold someone for an extra half-hour when there is a line waiting for tax preparation and only so many preparers meant that our own people would often avoid offering the benefit testing, so the software and time constraints were defeating us just as we were ready to go. We needed better, more effective tools to help us fight for citizen wealth.

Block thought it had found just that in a remarkable small company with a great name based in Austin, Texas, called Nets to Ladders, or more popularly N2L, founded and run by Marc Ferguson, who Bernie promptly started bringing to our meetings. According to ACORN Centers guru Jeff Karlson, N2L had a great program, and Bernie and Marc thought that we were close to being able to click a button and instantaneously move from the tax platform to the benefit screen, though that meant we would have to change to new tax preparation software. Block was willing to pay for the benefit screening software for all our states if we provided the list and moved forward in this direction. We instantly recognized that this opportunity could be huge.

The other problem was what to do with the "unbanked," as the financial services industry calls people who have no bank accounts. This is not really a surprise, since the business model of many large banks has shifted focus away from individual banking accounts. Many banks seem to have concluded that they lose money on the average minimum-balance customer and make money only on their other offerings. Companies such as Citi, for example, have increasingly moved away from consumer banking. Bank of America is one of the few majors that still seems to value individual accounts as part of its business model.[4]

In building citizen wealth all this matters in ways both large and small. In the tax business it matters because if someone does not have an account, then their refund cannot be electronically received by the filer after e-filing, causing more delays in receiving the return and sending too many of our people into the arms of the preparers who can offer an RAL. For several years we had worked with Citi to test systems with several of its lower-cost products to see if we could develop an alternative. Citi had some low-threshold, easy-to-access products that should have worked, but the problem that kept us crashing on the shoals was ironically Homeland Security. New banking regulations passed after 9/11 require a bank employee to be able to see the applicant personally to open an account. Citigroup tried various workarounds, including trying to schedule an employee for certain hours in several ACORN Centers in New York and Los Angeles, but we both knew from the beginning that it was unlikely to work, and it did not. Bernie and Block, on the other hand, had gotten an opinion directly from the Department of Homeland Security that they claimed would allow us to act as "agents" and would let us open accounts through a Visa card and the Block Bank right from the ACORN Centers. That would be a huge breakthrough.

Add a couple of hundred retooled computers, free software, a support team, and some money for outreach, and it seemed possible that this program would not only take the ACORN/H&R Block partnership to a new level, but help ACORN expand while doing the same for Block's new business model. We set a target to get to 1 million returns and benefits screenings in five years. Block felt it could add another 15 million returns by going deeper into its market base. This was exciting.

In building citizen wealth we could imagine the possibilities from the partnership in terms of radically increasing benefit participation. We talked about a three-way partnership among Block, ACORN, and N2L that would allow us to move state by state to help governors find the ways, means, and will power to bridge the technological, political, and often ideological gap to achieving full participation. The business model would allow it to pay off on a per-click basis, as Bernie and Marc argued. It was essentially a pay-for-performance model that would actually create an incentive for all of us to *increase* participation in benefit programs. The more people who qualified and accessed benefits, the more the model would pay off, and for the states it would be a win-win because it would mean more families with more income and wealth paying taxes and feeding dollars into the local economy, with the states reaping additional tax dollars. Austin King, the new director of the ACORN Financial Justice Center, found that the program could be developed using leftover TANF dollars that encouraged such investment, so there even seemed in some situations to be public resources to encourage such a program. Microsoft, another big player with a nonprofit/public division, was also interested in the screening application and how to make it work.

These were heady days. The ACORN Board of Directors was excited about this new direction for ACORN. It was also a new direction for Block. Mark Ernst, the CEO and chair of H&R Block's board, talked directly with Bernie and me during this period. He commented on the obvious: who would have believed that a relationship that began with street protests against predatory practices might evolve into a partnership where we would work together to create citizen wealth for millions of lower-income families. The change in the way the company was talking was so radical that some of the ACORN hands on the street were skeptical that the leopard could really have changed its spots in just three years. They were sure that Block Bank would be a ripoff in some way, but when we vetted and compared the account and credit options and our participation in the project with other offerings, Block's proposition was still better. As suspicious as we all were, we could not find a downside, and we desperately wanted to believe that working with a $4 billion company to increase benefits and wealth access was such a wild, innovative opportunity that we had to go the last inch to make it happen. It was full speed ahead to a business model that embraced creating wealth rather than picking pockets.

Wal-Mart and Mass Retail

There are certainly other enterprises, both large and small, for-profit and nonprofit, that have embraced low- and moderate-income families and individuals as their primary market, and despite their motivations could be considered as creating wealth rather than simply being predators. The biggest and perhaps the best on both sides of the line might be Wal-Mart and AARP.

The size and scale today of Wal-Mart is well known by everyone from schoolchildren on up, and the fact that 138 million Americans shop at Wal-Mart each week and eight out of ten Americans do so annually provides proof that most schoolchildren have also shared that grand experience.[5] Wal-Mart is not only the biggest firm of this generation and, seen strictly in economic terms, a huge success, it's also a highly controversial firm, largely due to its size. Wal-Mart now has over 6200 stores and employs 2.1 million "associates" worldwide; with 1.3 million associates working in America,[6] it's the largest private sector employer in the U.S. Its total revenue now passes $228 billion annually,[7] making the company one of the largest in the world.[8] Add the fact that Wal-Mart is also the largest private sector enterprise in Canada and Mexico and operates in thirteen other countries with another 620,000 employees, and it has become without doubt the largest private sector employer globally.[9] Sam Walton propelled a small country Arkansas department store into quite a legacy, making his family one of the wealthiest in the country as well.

Let's compare Wal-Mart with other major retail operations like Kmart and Target. Wal-Mart has specialized in selling to the $35,000-per-year family shopper, while Kmart and Target concentrate on families making $50,000 and Costco shoppers average $74,000.[10] Wal-Mart, like Block, has in recent years embarked on a highly publicized set of initiatives to attempt to go up-market with its brand and offerings, but has done so with little success. It's now focusing on its core customer base around the country, partly in response to the economic downturn, and is finally seeing some life in its laggard stock price, store-by-store sales, and other barometers of corporate health.

Wal-Mart's mission has been perfectly expressed in its previous slogan, "Always Low Prices." To deliver on that objective and to attract customers of modest means who are primarily motivated by pricing, the company created what is generally recognized as a state-of-the-art logistics and distribution system and the bedrock on which the company's price/sales leadership is anchored.

The company is controversial for many reasons, mostly because of its employment practices. Putting that aside for a minute, let us dispassionately look at the question of whether Wal-Mart in fact contributes to citizen wealth. Jason Furman makes a fascinating and controversial case for the Wal-Mart benefits in his paper "Wal-Mart: A Progressive Success Story."[11] As an economist, Furman addresses this question head on at the beginning of his piece: "There is little dispute that Wal-Mart's price reductions have benefited the 120 million American workers employed outside of the retail sector. Plausible estimates of the magnitude of the savings from Wal-Mart are enormous—a total of $263 billion in 2004, or $2329 per household."[12] He cites a 2005 study by Jerry Hausman and Ephraim Leibtag reporting that the impact of the big-box operations of all companies, including Wal-Mart (but largely driven by Wal-Mart's business model), was to reduce consumer spending on food by 20.2 percent—certainly a significant impact.[13] Furman argues that if you add indirect benefits of competition, Wal-Mart lowers annual food spending by another 4.8 percent, so that the benefit is "the equivalent of an additional $782 per household in 2003."[14] The families experiencing the maximum benefits from Wal-Mart–type operations are in the bottom three income quintiles, those who have incomes below $37,542, according to Furman's calculations.[15]

When we look at Wal-Mart's employment and labor relations practices, it is hard to maintain the same rosy view of the company's commitment to increasing citizen wealth. It is inarguable that Wal-Mart's compensation and benefit package pales in comparison to those of unionized firms, particularly in grocery stores whose workers belong to the United Food and Commercial Workers Union (UFCW), where wages may average as much as 20 percent more than Wal-Mart's in the same markets. We have already argued that there is a "union wage differential," and Wal-Mart is an excellent example of how and where it plays out.

Unfortunately, retail employment, despite its huge footprint in the service sector, is not widely unionized nationally. Union density in the retail sector is now estimated at 5.9 percent by the Bureau of Labor Statistics.[16] The problem represented by the actual worker wage levels at Wal-Mart in terms of our interest in citizen wealth is not simply one of comparing them to unionized workers. We must also put Wal-Mart in the context of the rest of the retail industry, and many argue that Wal-Mart's wages and benefits are comparable or at least not behind by such a significant level of magnitude as to offset other benefits of its business model for creating citizen wealth.[17]

I am a little more skeptical on this point than Professor Furman because he relies perhaps too heavily on Wal-Mart's self-validating claims about its average wages being near $9.70 per hour. He does cite the study done by Arindrajit Dube and Ken Jacobs,[18] based on hard data acquired through discovery in litigation, that the median hourly wage at Wal-Mart was just south of $9.00 per hour in 2001. In a study based on access to company-provided and accessible data filed in Florida in compliance with reporting to the state on the payment of unemployment insurance,[19] WARN (Wal-Mart Alliance for Reform Now) found that rather than paying $9.63 an hour in 2005, as Wal-Mart claimed, the company's actual average pay was closer to $6.35—at a time when the minimum wage in Florida was $6.15 per hour.[20] Wal-Mart tends to lump everyone together, including executives, store managers, and other supervisors, in its presentation of worker wages to the public, a practice that is deceptive.

There is also no excuse for some of Wal-Mart's labor relations policies, which seem to have included aggressive and longstanding discrimination involving women workers that could involve a liability of over a billion dollars (*Dukes* v. *Wal-Mart*, Case No 04-16688 [9th Cir. Feb. 6, 2007]).[21] Class action suits in Pennsylvania and other states charge that the company is responsible for working its associates off the clock, during breaks, and at other times, saving at least $50 million in this manner.[22] The aggressive and ideological anti-union stance of the company has resulted in findings of unfair labor practices, and the company is notorious for its willingness to close down entire departments throughout the company, as it did with its butcher shops when they organized in Dallas,[23] and has done more recently with an entire store, which was closed after union representation was certified in Quebec.[24] These actions have earned the company the enmity of organized labor and other concerned groups and have blinded many to the company's contributions in creating citizen wealth.[25]

Inarguably, though, the company created a business model that works, that focuses on how to deliver price, value, and service to lower-income consumers, and that where it operates has meant a difference in income, thereby resulting in opportunities to increase citizen wealth. Like H&R Block and many other enterprises, Wal-Mart could do much, much better, but that does not mean that it is not an outstanding success story in terms of creating both profits for the company and some real benefits for lower-income consumers.

AARP's Business

AARP (the American Association of Retired Persons) could not be a more different organization from Wal-Mart, but it is important to see

AARP as in fact a company, since although it's a nonprofit it also has an interesting business model and is an amazing success story. This is confusing because the AARP brand (and Wal-Mart could learn a lesson or two here!) is heavily identified with AARP being the gold standard as an advocate for elderly Americans. The organization has more than 35 million members, making it the largest membership organization in the country, second only perhaps to the Catholic Church.[26] Nonetheless, the AARP "organizing model" is part and parcel of its business model.

The organization was founded in 1958 by Ethel Percy Andrus, a retired Los Angeles school principal, who was no spring chicken at age seventy-two. The $50,000 in seed money to start the organization came from Leonard Davis, who was forty years younger at thirty-two and an insurance broker on the other side of the country in Poughkeepsie, New York. Davis had a plan and a purpose. Most health insurers at that time would not insure anyone over age sixty-five. Davis, though, had convinced Continental Casualty of Chicago to write policies for the fledgling AARP, thus combining a business model and an organizational model: AARP became the means by which the elderly could access health insurance, and Davis was the entry point to the insurers themselves and a large, untapped market of the elderly. The plan worked marvelously for both parties. Within five years AARP already had 750,000 members and by 1975, a dozen years later, had crossed the 10-million-member mark. Davis rolled with the tide and founded his own insurance company, Colonial Penn, as the numbers soared, replacing the original company. When AARP hit 10 million members, Davis and his company had revenues of $445 million, most of it from AARP members and had parlayed that first $50,000 grubstake into a personal fortune of $160 million.[27]

AARP has continued to grow steadily, and though its niche in insurance covering the elderly has now been filled by lots of companies, the organization is almost as well known for discounted prescription drug sales and other discounted products from trips and tours to financial advice. No small amount of the organization's revenue, now topping $1 billion,[28] comes from licensing its name and reputation as an advocate for the elderly. Investments are also huge revenue generators for this tax-exempt nonprofit. The AARP magazine, *Modern Maturity*, generates huge advertising revenues based on its captive-audience subscriber list. Recently, the magazine received wide publicity for a "new look" strategy that seems to have featured a nude or semi-nude Jamie Lee Curtis as she turned fifty.[29] The direct mail operation and the list database and collection are legendary for their effectiveness by the standards of either for-profit or nonprofit enterprises.

The entry-level dues payment for potential members over fifty years old began at around $5 a year and now is only $12.50 a year,[30] so the model is founded on a low threshold to membership. A tiny percentage of members are activists involved in advocacy, and a smaller percentage are involved in governance, but not necessarily any less so than in other well-known mass membership organizations such as unions. The organization has paid staff on the ground, usually in the capitals in all fifty states, supporting the local chapter structure and mobilizing around their legislative agenda. So though the organization could not be confused with a civil rights organization or local union or ACORN, there is also no question that it is a real organization rather than just a business scheme.

Evaluating the quality of its insurance or other business products is less easy. *Consumer Reports* has issued comparisons that have been both kind and unfavorable to AARP supplemental policies at different times. Certainly its current insurance partner, Universal Health,[31] is both well known and controversial itself. There seems little doubt, though, that AARP members/consumers believe that they are getting better value and savings on drugs and other programs, as well as other benefits that the organization is able to deliver because of its size and scale that far overshadow dues and are at the least competitive in the market.

Why Isn't the Low- and Moderate-Income Market Valued More Highly?

In some ways this question is less important to our purposes here. Some goods on Wal-Mart shelves made in China may not be as high in quality as an equivalent product sold at a high-end retail outlet elsewhere. But if the price is reasonable and the quality acceptable, and certainly that is the case with food, then Wal-Mart's impact on citizen wealth is substantial. Similarly with AARP: if good value is being given relative to price to elderly citizens, who are most at risk around issues of citizen wealth, since they are usually in the position of having to protect wealth to provide for themselves and future intergenerational transfers, then the positive impact on citizen wealth is significant.

The H&R Block theory seemed right. Block had a reliable customer base, and if that base had more income the company would do better as a "trusted adviser" on many fronts rather than as a predator. Wal-Mart was right as well. Once it had proven to its customers that it had the lowest prices and offered the best value for money, there were thousands of items that it could sell lower-income and working families once they were in the store and shopping. AARP discovered the same formula because it was seen as standing up for elderly citizens and consumers and could increase both its membership base and its customer base for discount health, insurance, tours, and other products the elderly found attractive.

We have seen this before as banks, kicking and screaming, finally came to an uneasy peace with the Community Reinvestment Act and have made scads of money by doing so. Admittedly, the density of home ownership, and therefore asset accumulation among the poor, is still shamefully low, at only one in five lower-income families, for a country that touts home ownership as a cornerstone of the American dream.[32] But banks would seem to be in the catbird seat in building an effective business model for many other financial services.

In fact, some experts are doing everything but standing on Park Avenue in front of the ornate lobby of Citi headquarters and waving banners saying "Make Money on the Poor Now!" A study recently indicated that there are 22 million households—20 percent of all U.S. households—without a bank account.[33]

Adding the unbanked to the number of subprime credit customers among the LMI could push the number of households to 40 percent, or between 30 million and 40 million "who spend at least 2% of their income on basic financial services." This vast untapped market "could be worth $4 billion to $9 billion in revenues."[34]

Hello out there, where are you?!

Financial Products for the LMI Market

Stored value cards (SVDs) are one product that has been tailored to this constituency by some companies and is widely used as an alternative to banking, especially by young adults. Similar to prepaid cards, the risk for financial institutions is minuscule since a consumer is loading the card with cash money or a direct transfer from a paycheck or other means. I did not include SVDs when looking at whether a family could build assets through debt, because these cards in many ways are less about debt than simply filling a market niche by serving the unbanked.

In fact, some of these cards accelerate debt because they charge transaction costs that can be predatory. We had to walk away from our friend Russell Simmons, the hip-hop impresario and entrepreneur, for exactly that reason when he tried to convince us that his card was "the bomb." We were similarly unhappy to see Jackson Hewitt try to use its card as a receptacle for tax refunds in some areas where the Russell Simmons "brand" was thought to attract our people. Again, the potential market for such cards is huge. In 2005 industry estimates indicated that there were then 2000 or more different programs with 7 million Visa- or MasterCard-branded cards.[35] The report indicated that the industry expected there to be 49 million users by 2008.[36] Transactions, which once again are how the companies make their money in this business model, were expected to "reach over $72 billion."[37]

A company that did move forward with this business model was NetSpend, which was founded in 1999 in Austin, Texas, by Roy and Bernard Sosa to process prepaid and stored value cards.[38] NetSpend has been a success story and now claims 1 million cardholders, who have loaded more than $4 billion onto their cards. People get the cards through grocery stores and check-cashing outlets, which I don't like, but as Chris Rock famously said, "I understand." But stepping into the arena of citizen wealth, NetSpend began an interesting program called "All-Access National Savings Program" that allowed cardholders to move money into interest-bearing savings accounts through a transfer from their prepaid debit cards, either on a regular, automatic basis or as a one-time transaction. The savings accounts earn interest and are held at Inter National Bank in Texas, and the only pop on the account is when the cardholder moves to withdraw, but there is no transaction charge on funds coming into savings.

More recently, NetSpend in 2007 increased the interest rate to 5 percent as a promotion in order to drive more of its customers into savings accounts. Proving that such a business model is attractive, NetSpend was close to being acquired by the credit card and banking giant CapitalOne. Although the merger was canceled in 2008, the strategic partnership between the two companies has been continued and CapitalOne has increased its investment, so who knows what the future might hold as CapitalOne looks at replicating this model on a larger scale.

Another interesting incentive that has been widely discussed focuses on "reward points" along the same model as frequent flyer awards. Diversion of reward points into savings rather than increased consumption and moving the money into tax-free 529 college savings programs grew from 1999 to 2003 from $1 billion to $35 billion, which also could be a strong step toward citizen wealth as an investment in more training or the next generation's educational needs.[39]

This is an intriguing, though untested, prospect, just as the H&R Block bank concept of acting as a source of short-term consumer loans in response to FDIC Chairman Sheila Bair's directive was encouraging, in order to provide competition with payday lenders. However, much work needs to be done. Bair showed real leadership on this issue in the summer of 2007, laying out a direct challenge: "Many borrowers who use payday loans have a checking account and a steady paycheck, so why aren't they borrowing from their bankers?"[40] She posed exactly the right question. Why are regular banks not stepping up to deal with short-term consumer loans for either their own customers or customers who are in every way bankable? The FDIC guidelines that slapped at payday lending and sought to create competition in this area involved setting "reasonable interest rates below 36 percent, low origination fees, and repayment periods longer than a single pay period." Additionally, the FDIC instruction supported "including an 'automatic' savings component to help small-loan borrowers start a savings account at the bank."[41] Such a program would actually convert a predatory situation into a real opportunity for a family to create citizen wealth, and that is a great policy. The FDIC announced a two-year pilot to showcase "best practices" among any banks that take on the challenge to meet the proven, billion-dollar demand for "low-cost, small-dollar loans."[42] "It is my hope that, over the next few years, responsibly priced small-dollar loans will become a staple offering among our nation's banks," Bair said.[43]

Hear, hear! I for one hope it is a long line, but a year later I am hard pressed to name a handful of banks that have stepped forward to meet the challenge. For the most part we are knocking at the door without being able to break through with large-scale buy-in from financial institutions. The Center for Financial Services Innovation (CFSI) draws the issue squarely in two different critiques of its own industry, making this report as valuable as a look over the transom. First, looking at the need for increased financial education that could encourage the use and matching of IDAs,[44] CFSI stresses that "aside from a handful of experiments around less costly, web-based delivery methods, no one has figured out how to provide the financial education component at scale."[45] The report further calls the banks to task for both a lack of attentiveness and a fundamental antipathy to the low- and moderate-income market: Banks have "overlooked the corresponding savings and investment opportunities" because of "the lack of cross-divisional communication in financial institutions [that] has made them ineffective champions for implementing a broader array of financial services. Connecting both sides of the bank is critical to catalyzing new thinking and new strategies."[46] Quite right!

If companies can see and prove that there is money to be made by doing the right thing even in a highly competitive environment, then why are not more of them doing it? And how can forces in the community push firms in the right direction, especially toward partnerships to build citizen wealth?

12

Bringing Citizens into the Wealth-Building Process

Families are legally entitled to receive a wide range of benefits created by governments to increase wealth, diminish poverty, and make everything about life simply better for the citizens of this great country. It's therefore hard for me to understand why government agencies are not held accountable for the actual delivery of these services and benefits to American families.

There is a simple answer, of course, and I have stumbled on it over and over during more than forty years as an organizer: government is not citizen centered. In fact, government sometimes seems to exist for its own perpetuation rather than to provide services to citizens and to respond to their needs. That may not correspond to the rhetoric of politicians, bureaucrats, and officials of one stripe or another, but it is the reality, and it is at the heart of the problem of creating citizen wealth.

Let's talk now about how we can rethink this proposition and create a citizen-centered system that actually works to help citizens access services and benefits that have been designed for them. How hard can this be in our high-tech, can-do society? Nonetheless, once again the burden seems to rest on the victims of the initial indifference to solve the problem, while government agencies and others watch from the sidelines. Hopefully, we will find them eventually ready to get in the game.

Whose Job Is It?

In looking at the problem of accessing eligible benefits I was struck by a clear statement of the obvious in a July 2005 report by the Family Strengthening Policy Center: "In a very real sense, it is no one's job to help an individual or family presenting itself to a public or private agency to access the full range of benefits and supports it may need. Each agency has its specialty and is held accountable for providing specific services, no more, no less. Veering off to help a client or family learn about the broader range of supports available to it has historically been time-consuming, labor-intensive, and an unreimbursed activity."[1]

Bang! You can hear the nail being hit on the head as you imagine a family or anyone else trying to figure out a way to find a path through the alphabet soup of government agencies and programs (IRS, USDA, WIC, EITC, LIHEAP, SCHIP) in the hope that there might be something at the end of the rainbow. This is especially true when studies continually find that a major part of the problem in increasing participation is in fact disinformation or misinformation given to citizens about whether they are eligible and whether applying is worth their while. An important breakthrough in federal thinking now incorporated on the websites of many agencies is a USDA benefits calculator that seeks to surprise citizens by letting them know that they could actually get more benefits than they might have thought.[2] Of course, we have to get that family to a computer somehow, which can seem like imagining how to fit dancing shoes on an elephant.

But let's not be discouraged. We are so close to being able to solve this problem, partially by creating a powerful new platform to access benefits with the development of new technology. If we can create such a platform, it will be an easier step to deliver access to that technology to citizens.

The technological opportunity is available within the applications that companies like Nets to Ladders are constructing now in bits and pieces. These screening tools break down the bureaucratic barriers between agencies and programs and create a paradigm that is user friendly and citizen centered in the terms that we need to achieve.

Other companies are already working on similar projects in the fragmented way that these things happen. The Philadelphia-based Benefit Bank is slowly developing a state-by-state for-profit model.

Community Catalyst in Boston has put together some pieces. The Robin Hood Foundation and Atlantic Philanthropies have joined to finance SingleStop in New York in its plans to scale up solutions in the Middle Atlantic region. There is little collaboration among these efforts, however, and problematically in my view almost no governmental investment in or commitment to their success.

The Building Blocks of a New Platform

The building blocks of the new model are several. First, initial screening and tax preparation along the lines that the ACORN Centers have developed is certainly the most accessible entry point.

Second, the application needs to get into the system when the screen determines eligibility. On the core programs in the N2L system an application for many of the basic programs can be downloaded and printed right there for completion and delivery. This is not really that much of a breakthrough, since all fifty states have created the facilities on their websites that let users download and print applications.[3] Time and other paperwork submissions are still obstacles, of course. Even more promising and powerful are online application systems that would let the application be immediately submitted as part of a "one-stop shopping" system. As I write, there are only tentative steps in this direction, with only a handful of states having approved the procedures.[4]

Streamlining a citizen-centered application system also needs to embrace a document scanning and retention program for the poor. This point is obvious, but that does not mean that any program currently focuses on making this happen, at least to my knowledge. ACORN's national headquarters had been in New Orleans since 1978, but we were taught this lesson as we lived through Hurricane Katrina in August 2005 with our 9,000 member families in the city. When the levees broke many entire neighborhoods were flooded out with a suddenness that allowed no preparation,[5] and tens of thousands of families lost everything, including all of their personal records. Creating scanning and document retention capabilities through the ACORN Centers is one of the mainstays of our program, but this needs to be a national priority. The costs are relatively trivial on an individual basis, but like the giant Google project of scanning entire libraries, everything takes time and money, and the labor necessary to help build citizen wealth cannot be free. But we could provide a vital service by scanning critical documents, insurance papers, home titles, birth certificates, tax returns, W-2s, baptismal records, property tax assessments, health and dental records, school records, and other information and putting them on a thumb-drive or CD. Individuals or families could walk away with their information secure while maintaining it on a protected server in case something else happens or it gets lost. The next step would be getting government agencies to recognize the validity of the scanned document as part of the online application process so that we could achieve some synchronization between the screened recognition of eligibility and the full completion and submission of the application.

Other tweaks in the system that could help might be video camera linkages between the applicant's computer and the agency in the presence of an advocate for assistance. At the least, interactive programs in various languages could be critical. Once again, we believe that if we have the will we can find a way to bridge the digital divide.

Third, the screening and the application process has to be comprehensive and weld together *all* programs, large and small, that might fit the family if we are to make the platform as powerful as we need it to be to create citizen wealth. At various times the ACORN Center system has been able to access and screen for up to fifteen programs, but this capability needs to be more extensive to be truly robust.

Adding Branches to the Tree

Here is an example of how robust I think it should be. A number of colleges have over the last several years ratcheted up costs for higher education in double digits, far surpassing the rate of inflation. They did this even while they were sitting on endowments in the millions and sometimes billions of dollars. However, some of them have announced that they will try to broaden the income mix of their student populations by giving virtually full-ride scholarships to some students from families making less than $50,000 or $100,000 a year. In the pages of the *New York Times* and elsewhere college administrators wondered how they would find the "deserving poor" ready to go to Harvard, Yale, and elsewhere out in the countryside. Why would we not screen families for this type of program as well? Certainly, a ticket to an Ivy League college is almost certainly as good as winning the lottery for many young people if the reports of average salaries for their graduates are accurate. Why not screen for all families that have high school juniors with high grade averages as they sit in ACORN Centers or at computers wherever they are, forwarding contact information to these colleges and letting them recruit and mean it rather than sitting back and seeing what comes in over their transom on the tree-lined quad.

There is a program in San Francisco that helps lower-income families pay for mandatory car seats. Put it in.

There are scholarships that are only available for people from certain neighborhoods or who are members of particular churches or ethnic groups. Put them in.

Some citizens are not registered to vote. Register them right there. Send them out ready to vote on the next election day.

The point is building a platform powerful enough to allow for as many additions as become available—a strong trunk with unlimited room for branches. Where there is an income test requiring an application we need to create the software applications that can sort through all of the possibilities from a citizen-centered or user-friendly perspective and spit out the opportunities for a family to achieve citizen wealth.

Using a Captive Audience

The other point has to be full utilization of the captive audience. The software is worthless unless we can put people's bottoms in the chair in front of the computer, whether at the ACORN Centers or in libraries, grocery stores, hospital waiting rooms, or government offices. It also goes without saying that this is America, so the time required to be in the chair cannot be too long.

Besides the other arguments made earlier about the need for outreach and accessibility, it would be helpful if we could add a couple of incentives to the platform and to the outreach work. Continuing to link access, as the ACORN Centers do, with tax preparation may provide advantages here.

An interesting experiment was done by a highly regarded community bank, Chicago's ShoreBank (formerly South Shore Bank) and the Center for Economic Progress (CEP, formerly the Center for Law and Human Services) in 1999. CEP did tax work onsite twice a week at a ShoreBank office providing free tax services for EITC-eligible families. ShoreBank created an account called the Extra Credit Savings Program

(ESCP). The trick—and incentive—was that the ESCP would "provide low-cost bank accounts to those who arrange for direct deposit of tax refunds and offers a small incentive payment in these accounts."[6] The account had some nice features, including market-rate interest rates and a no-fee ATM card, and account holders would receive a 10 percent bonus on any money remaining in the account at the end of the year up to a cap of $100, so there were all of the features of an incentive program for both creating banking access and encouraging savings. In the report on the experiment's first year the results were somewhat negligible and hard to fully assess, based on the limited outreach, follow-up, and education around the benefits of the program and even the existence of the incentive itself. In reality, some clients remembered the program incentive and it mattered to them, and some got it and some did not, but the design of the program holds promise for more work and adaptation with potentially good results in building citizen wealth if applied differently and more widely.

Similarly, H&R Block put together a matching program to encourage similar savings of refund dollars in New York City in 2004 and the results were very strong, with all sides trumpeting the success of this novel incentive program.[7] After Block gained a charter for its own bank, it offered an "Emerald Card" and a bank account in conjunction with tax returns it prepared. Block enrolled several million people in the first year of the program, with about 10 percent retaining the accounts long term even after using them to receive their returns.[8]

The other large incentives are in individual development accounts, or IDAs. The costs of most of these proposals are not trivial, because the level of matching and fund accounting is more significant than required by these other trials and pilots. Additionally, most of the IDAs, true to their names, are designed for special savings purposes like home purchases, business or training investments, and other large purchases. Incentives are incentives, though, and inarguably the push toward citizen wealth is more likely to be successful if incentives help to point the way.

Programs like the ACORN Centers are already set up with software made of bailing wire and chewing gum to be able to screen for IDAs in addition to Food Stamps, Medicaid, WIC, SCHIP, TANF, LIHEAP, childcare subsidies, weatherization assistance, local energy assistance programs, voter registration, and tuition assistance, as well as referrals for home buyer counseling or loan modification assistance for families facing foreclosure. Every participant in the ACORN Centers is also enrolled as a "provisional" member of ACORN, meaning that they are given a free introductory membership in order to get them into the database to receive continued information, referrals, and updates, get alerts through the ACORN Call Center in New Orleans of new programs, and set times and appointments for coming taxes, as well as access news about what may be happening in their neighborhoods and opportunities to get involved in their local community organization. These kinds of value-added community-based support programs can assist in both outreach and continued construction of citizen wealth through community for lower-income and working families. In 2008 ACORN Centers were running in almost all of the ninety-five ACORN offices in the United States and enabling 50,000 tax returns to be filed in the first year of the H&R Block/ACORN partnership in this new era.

The challenge for the ACORN Centers, like those of so many other community-based efforts, is how to get full alignment across all of its work in order to increase the traffic dramatically into the ACORN Centers on a year-round basis. Within ACORN's current outreach capacity there are more than 2 million visits a year through community work, more than 1.5 million registered to vote during the 2008 election cycle, almost 500,000 who are contacted through housing and foreclosure avoidance programs, more than 100,000 daily listeners to one of the associated radio stations working with ACORN in Dallas and Little Rock, but only 50,000 actual tax returns filed annually through the ACORN Centers. Even a smaller number of these are spending the extra time to get screened for benefits. In a microcosm, the challenge for Diné Butler, Jeff Karlson, and the ACORN Center local directors is the same for America at large. How do they align more of the huge outreach they are doing and drive the traffic into their own offices and centers? If they are contacting 4 million to 5 million lower-income families a year, only about 1 percent are actually getting through the door and into the ACORN Center program.

This is part of the challenge of all discretionary or volunteer outreach designed to increase citizen wealth. As we noted earlier, in America today it is no one's job. Until we make creating citizen wealth everyone's job, regardless of government disinclination or the coordination and synchronization challenges faced by hundreds of community groups and other sources of support and good will, change will not come and citizen wealth will not be created.

It really is as simple as that.

13

The Future of Citizen Wealth

The potential to create citizen wealth is almost limitless. The limits are in fact not simply the size of the federal or state treasuries, and we have now learned that there really *are* no limits when it comes to something the government *wants* to do, so perhaps we have to make government *want* families to have financial security. Doubtless, more money invested in citizen wealth or asset-building strategies for lower- and working-income families would help. The government is already spending a truckload on asset building, more even than it is spending on war. A central problem is how to get government to spend the money well and, perhaps more to the point, how to force government to spend it right so that the right people benefit from all this investment in citizen wealth. That is not happening now.

Current Government Spending on Citizen Wealth

Estimates as current as 2006 indicate that asset-building incentives at the federal level alone carried a price tag of $367 billion for FY 2005.[1] The money in many cases takes the form of tax credits or tax incentives in four categories:[2]

- Savings and investment: $125.43 billion
- Retirement: $124.40 billion
- Home ownership: $116.55 billion
- Small business development $ .65 billion

We are looking at a lot of money, but the problem is determining whose assets are being developed with these huge expenditures and then asking whether those are the people who really need this kind of help from the federal government.

Lets look at home ownership first. The list includes some affordable housing programs and certainly Community Development Block Grants (CDBGs), which are nominally intended for low- and moderate-income (LMI) areas by HUD regulation, but that basket totals less than $1 billion. The big money is in tax subsidies: $72.6 billion from the deduction for mortgage interest, almost $23 billion from excluding capital gains on sales of your main house (the phrase *main house* already tells you where this is going), $19.6 billion from allowing you to deduct property taxes, and just shy of a billion from letting you exclude interest on state and local bonds for owner-occupied housing.[3]

So who wins in government asset-building investments? Turns out that the richest 10 percent of taxpayers capture almost 60 percent of the benefits, and the entire bottom *half* of taxpayers receive less than 3 percent of these benefits.[4] The 2002 report of President Bush's Advisory Panel on Federal Taxes notes that 55 percent of the mortgage deduction benefit goes into the happy hands of taxpayers topping $100,000 per year. Of this amount, almost $20 billion, the panel found that the bottom *half* of the taxpayers got about a half-billion dollars' worth of benefits.[5] In short, the government is providing a mountain of money but is certainly not moving to increase citizen wealth for the bottom half of our citizens.

We all concede that savings are critical in building citizen wealth, but here too the investment by the federal government seems skewed away from low- and moderate-income families rather than toward them. There is some money in refugee resettlement and in the Assets for Independence Act,[6] but the big-ticket appropriations are specialized tax breaks that deal with estates ($38 billion), gifts ($4.6 billion), reduced rates on capital gains ($57.8 billion), and the exclusion of investment income on life insurance and annuities, which is worth $25 billion in tax forgiveness for somebody. And the "somebody" is even more disproportionately in the higher strata, with 95 percent of the benefit going to 10 percent of the earners (those with incomes of at least $133,000). The poorest 30 percent of households, those with incomes less than $30,000, received a benefit of less than $5.00

from all these measures.[7] Yes, that's not a typo: $5.00. Another $124 billion subsidizes retirement funds through employers: individual retirement accounts (IRAs), Keogh plans, and tax credits in this area, but lower-income families do not reap much benefit in accumulating citizen wealth in this area either, because they are naturally less likely to save because they have a thinner income base, and they are also less likely to work for employers who offer these benefits. Lastly, about $600 million in this big pot amortizes business startup costs for largely middle-income applicants and less than $50 million to encourage lower-income families to go into business development. The Small Business Administration (SBA) is involved in micro lending and in fact invested about $1 million in that way in FY2005, hardly enough to cover the lowest bet on the table.[8]

Who benefits? This report is telling when it says that "the poorest fifth of the population get, on average, $3 in benefits from these policies, while the wealthiest 1% enjoy, on average, $57,673. Households with incomes of $1 million or more receive an average benefit of $169,150."[9] On one hand, $3 for 20 percent of American taxpayers, and on the other hand $169,150 per year for 1 percent of the taxpayers.

In short, precious federal tax dollars are being invested in citizen wealth, but the investment is going to those citizens who are already at the top, and that is where it is staying. There is little or no pretense that wealth is ever going to trickle down.

Full participation in all entitlements by all eligible citizens would also be a huge breakthrough, as we have discussed repeatedly. The Clinton administration ratcheted up the level of support, particularly to working families, from 1996 to 2001. These benefits could make all the difference in the world. In 2002, for example, "a single parent with two children earning $10,000 (a full-time job at minimum wage)[10] could have received about $23,600 in work support (including childcare subsidies of $12,000 for two young children, Medicaid for the parent and both children, food stamps, and the EITC."[11] The family of three would then have an income of $33,600 and be on their way to citizen wealth.

Fixing What Is Broken
Of course, once again reality intrudes. Most families do not receive the full package of entitlements and in fact are often discouraged from

doing so. In fact, "even among the working poor—[those with] income below the federal poverty level, families most clearly within all of the programs' income eligibility ranges—only 7 percent received all four supports in 2002."[12] Our distribution system is totally broken right at the door of the families that need the programs the most.

Part of the reason lies in the classic problem of "herding cats." The exception is the EITC, which, to give the devil his due, is a single consistent system within the IRS, no matter how passive the IRS might be in promoting participation. The rules vary wildly from state to state for the rest of these work support programs. Throw in the fact that this can also go "Helter Skelter" as the states mix and match children's ages, family expenses, immigrant status, and other factors, and the problem is daunting.

This confusion has to change, and the federal government needs to work with the states to streamline these programs and make them more coherent and consistent. There is a problem, though, in that some states do better than the federal government, and in building citizen wealth we absolutely cannot allow ourselves to go backward by one dollar. The software applications that many companies are developing to increase electronic screening and access will sand down the rough edges of varying state programs, though the bottom line of the system of citizen wealth cannot be playing "gotcha" with eligible families and seeing if they can make it through the maze.

We also need a full assault from every quarter, and in my mind that includes not discouraging big companies in the service sector that are large employers of lower-wage workers in the hospitality and hotel sector, among cleaners and janitors, among part-time workers and lower-wage workers in healthcare and daycare, in retail employment, and on and on. We need the companies to take an affirmative role in being way stations to sign up their workers to maximize their benefits. For example, rather than castigating Wal-Mart because a high percentage of its workers access such benefits, we need to encourage and applaud Wal-Mart's efforts to get its workers (associates) to apply.

Wal-Mart might even have a model here that could work. In many stores, especially in low-unemployment areas, there is a computer in the very front of the store so that anyone can mosey on up and apply immediately for a job with Wal-Mart! How about a computer that allows any of Wal-Mart's 128 million weekly customers to apply for benefits right there as well? How about a similar piece of software in the back next to the employee time cards that lets all of the workers self-screen with a set of easy prompts as directions and an automatic benefits calculator to help them through the program? Contrary to my friends and colleagues in the Wal-Mart accountability brigade (and I stand second to none of them!), it is not a public subsidy of Wal-Mart when lower-wage Wal-Mart workers get the government benefits they are entitled to. It is an investment in those workers' path to citizen wealth.

Getting in Gear

If I can say that about Wal-Mart, then you know there is no limit to what I believe that you should do as well.

Forty years ago one of the most interesting things I learned (and taught!) as an organizer for welfare rights was the simple power of personal advocacy, or what we called "grievances" when I began work in Springfield, Massachusetts. The members, welfare recipients themselves, would agree to learn as much as they could about the welfare system and the welfare manuals, and the organization would help do training, as would more senior and experienced leaders who knew the system. These grievance committees and their members would do two types of things, both of which were invaluable. They would schedule time with other applicants, mostly women with children trying to get Aid to Families with Dependent Children (AFDC, or welfare as we used to know it), to go with them in person to navigate the system, to sit with them when they talked to the caseworker, and by hook or crook to get them on the aid rolls.

The other thing they would do was perhaps even more powerful: set up tables or plant themselves in the huge waiting room of the Springfield welfare office, which had been an old supermarket at the top of the Hill, the core of the African American community in that city, and, with their NWRO buttons on, talk to people as they came in about how to make it through the often byzantine application system. This was outreach, perhaps, but it was almost more like "in-reach," right there on the spot where organizers could fully engage and assist people in trying to understand and access the system.

This strategy was not particularly revolutionary or innovative, of course. My years directing a local labor union with the Service Employees have allowed me to both see (and build) the same systems that are commonplace and part of the expected practice for unions and particularly union stewards in workplaces. Unions are only as strong as their stewards and members on the floor of the employer's establishment or wherever the worksite might be. For the most part, outside of the old-line industrial unions, stewards are unpaid rank-and-file members who know the company, not the contract or the rules and regulations that go with making work survivable and fair on that jobsite, and who simply stand for justice and fairness for their co-workers on the job.

In the wake of Katrina, I have seen some of the same grit and spirit in young people, church groups, and other volunteers who have trooped down to New Orleans regularly since the storm hit in 2005 to help with ACORN's gutting program or do park cleanups, or paint houses being rehabbed in Lower 9th Ward or anywhere there might be a need. Sometimes they show up in ones and twos during spring or year-end breaks and come back from year to year with other schoolmates or clubs. Sometimes they show up by the hundreds and thousands, and the ACORN hurricane recovery crews (because this is still a daily experience) tear their hair out accommodating the huge numbers and supplying the tools and materials to make their time and effort valuable.

A lot of these volunteers are students. New Orleans has fortunately become a Mecca for young people trying to make a difference and wanting to get in on the ground floor of helping rebuild a great American city. But a lot of the people we see are simply people of good will. They simply want to help. They show up in their RVs like Clarence Whelan and his wife did, saying that he was a retired carpenter and asking how he could help. Or Ray Russell, the brother of an old friend, who had been an electrician in North Carolina and came back to the city to what could be done and has now been here almost three years. Or Dean Hubbard, a friend and former Sarah Lawrence professor, who comes down with his church group for one week every year and lends a hand.

Part of the crisis of Katrina was a crisis of citizen wealth. Thousands of families lacked the wherewithal to leave, or if they could leave, then to come back, or if they were able to come back, then to rebuild, in the vicious cycle that has beset one of the world's great cities—but also a city that had been one of the poorest in America and almost two-thirds African American at the time Katrina struck. We need this same spirit of good will and community to take root not only in New Orleans, though God knows we still need all the help we can get here, but everywhere else in the country when it comes to moving forward on citizen wealth.

We need an army of volunteers who make citizen wealth their mission and stand just as those welfare moms did right there in the centers until others get help or just as those union stewards stand next to a colleague with a beef and make sure it all gets settled right. This is not rocket science. No matter how complex local, state, and federal bureaucrats make the rules, regular people can still read them and wend their way through them, and being in the right place at the right time can make the difference in whether or not we get maximum eligible participation. This is something that students could do right where they live or go to school. This is something that seniors could do right where they live or travel. This is something that union stewards should be doing, and schoolteachers, and church people. This is also something that should be part of the human resources program in hospitals, hotels, restaurants, grocery and retail stores, janitorial companies, home health and daycare companies, nonprofits and for-profits, and, OK, you get the message: This is something that should become part of the standard package and not just with a leaflet, but with real help.

This same army needs not only to stand with their neighbors and lend a hand, but also needs to stand up to the government and elected officials at all levels and demand real programs to increase citizen wealth and real value for citizens from the expenditures already being made. I am not unrealistic. We are not going to see repeal of something like mortgage interest rate reductions for taxpayers making more than $100,000 or $200,000 any time soon, but it is both fair and urgent for all citizens to ask that the government mean what it says and actually deliver citizen wealth programs to lower-income and working families and not simply divert these precious resources to upper-income families who in the main are well on their way to developing citizen wealth on their own, thank you.

I have been skeptical about whether one can really build citizen wealth through using credit and taking on debt, but ironically that seems to be exactly the government's program. One estimate is that for every $1 that the government currently spends to actually help people build assets, it is dwarfed by the $582 being provided in the form of tax credits and revenue losses to the federal treasury to "encourage" (upper-class) citizen wealth.[13] This seems backward, and whether backward or not, it simply is not working by any of the measures we have examined repeatedly in this book. Lower-income and working families, especially those eligible for EITC, have no way to use a tax credit that does not convert into cash. A credit of this type therefore does nothing to move such a family toward more wealth.

In order to increase family security, even at the most minimal levels of what we are defining as citizen wealth, we have to be able to move away from cynicism at that level. We need to adjust policies to allow retention of more assets before qualification for benefits and entitlements, similar to the steps already taken around IDAs. Our policies have to more often reflect an open hand and less a tight fist.

When we talk to our governmental and elected officials we need to persuade them begin to backbone-up against the small Taliban caves full of haters who are convinced that every penny a family receives is not a step toward family security and a better America, but something wrested personally from their pockets. *It absolutely is not.* In fact, as we have seen, unless there is a tax credit in their pockets, it is nothing to them at all—at least personally—and it is certainly not the government spending their "precious tax dollar," since the government is hardly spending even that much when compared with other subsidies. There are these people at large in the land, and they have their obsessions and their rages, but as they rage the government hides from them by sleight of hand that it is giving away the store to the top 1 percent, and 10 percent, and 30 percent of American families, and not doing anywhere near the job that needs to be done for the bottom 50 percent of Americans.

Building the Citizen Wealth Campaign

There are huge roles in the campaign for citizen wealth for both nonprofit organizations and the most dollar-driven, profit-motivated firm, and it is in their interests to see their members or clients, or customers for that matter, achieve more income and begin to build real wealth. The ACORN Centers that we have discussed at length are a good model of combining tax and benefit access with a host of other services and supports in a one-stop-shopping system for lower-income and working families, and there are other programs like CEP in Chicago, FoodChange in New York City, and Community Catalyst in Boston that are breaking new ground in many of these areas. This is a powerful platform whose time is coming soon with or without government making it easier to access and quicker to implement.

There are huge opportunities for business models that increase wealth, but there are never guarantees that eliminate all risk, whether for nonprofits or for-profit enterprises. Wal-Mart certainly created one of the world's largest companies by focusing on low prices and attracting lower-income consumers. Too many predators continue to dominate this market, but as we see in fields from tax preparation to banking there are signs of change that could be significant. There just needs to be so much more. Companies need to see increasing citizen wealth as part of their social responsibility and civic obligation.

I talked last year in New York to a representative of a huge investment house in a meeting only a couple of yards off Wall Street. The executive visiting with me bemoaned the time it took to be trained in doing tax preparation and how that did not work for the employees they were marshalling to volunteer. There is a role, though, both within their own business and throughout the city in pushing assistance and advocating to bring thousands and millions into the system. I could see his eyes glaze when I described the few hours it would take to spend the extra time with people in the waiting rooms of the ACORN Centers or other locations and the difference in citizen wealth it could make. There was little fancy or exciting in the picture I laid out for him, it seemed, but making that very real impact is where he would have to find the thrill.

We also need to alter dramatically public and private programs and policies in order to create citizen wealth. We could make a long list, but even before doing so we need to start by sanding down all of the rough spots in what we have now. Without a single new law or spending a single new penny, we could make a huge difference in citizen wealth if we could *rationalize* the regulations so that they reflected some standardization and uniformity. There are too many fielder's[10] choices being played in state after state that create barriers to access and participation in too many programs. Far be it from me to advocate that states should not be able to improve benefits and create experiments that increase citizen wealth, but they should all be working from the same playbook. For all of my criticism of the IRS and its lack of meaningful outreach around EITC, at least there is no question anywhere in the country about how EITC works, who is eligible, and what you have to do to help someone access the benefit. It's therefore not surprising that the program actually works. There are, sadly, way too few programs about which that simple statement can be made.

Many states are so committed to these programs not being a "gimme" that they have made them into a "gotcha." This is not the way to achieve citizen wealth for lower-income and working families. There needs to be a top-to-bottom attitude adjustment that is citizen centered and creates value and wealth for the priceless people of our country.

I actually believe that if we join together to build a campaign to achieve citizen wealth by each stepping forward and doing our part, then we can create through such a movement pressure on state and local authorities to do the right thing. Even after forty years as an organizer working in the vineyards of social and economic change, with all of the cynicism that can bring and the jaded perspectives about governments, business, and even some people that can arise, I really believe that, everything being equal, people really want to do the right thing and feel better for it. The problem is at the heart of the task of making sure that everything is made equal. Doing so takes masses of people, teeming hordes of people, but once assembled and organized they are an irresistible force that moves even the most immovable object.

That has to happen. And when it happens, not only will the rules of the road for achieving citizen wealth become clear and transparent and therefore more accessible, but it will be worth the time and energy to talk to our elected officials and all of the big whoops from the statehouse to the White House about putting the dollars down to actually build citizen wealth rather than just shuffling this and that around in the name of a response without doing the work of engaging in real solutions.

There are lots of great ideas and innovations in both predictable and, as we found with our friends at H&R Block, even surprising places. We have discussed a number of them here. If we can build this campaign together, my bet is that another hundred or more ideas about how to build citizen wealth will spring up within minutes and days.

None of this will be easy.

In fact, there is even another story within the story of ACORN's partnership with H&R Block. In the fall of 2007, as a backdrop to the discussions we were having about a new partnership between Block and the ACORN Centers and a new business model for both of us to achieve maximum eligible participation, there was also a boardroom drama at play involving the former head of the SEC, Richard Breeden, and H&R Block CEO Mark Ernst.

More than once after I read something in the business press, I would ask Bernie, "What's up? Should I be following this and worrying about it?" Inevitably, he would reassure me that this was backstage and would not affect what we were doing. He believed that, and so did I. Then Breeden managed to get elected to the board and bring a couple of his colleagues along with him in a power play. Ernst hung on for a while, but there was death in the air, and before long Breeden was the new chairman, Ernst was landing in Kansas City with a severance parachute, and the world of Block was upside down. Before long Bernie was swept clean by the new broom as well. The culprit was not the new business model. Ironically, Ernst was felled by the irascible bunch at Option One and the subprime horse they rode in on. Block's inability to even fire-sale Option One after the implosion of the subprime industry had collected another casualty.

In the real world there are no fairy-tale endings, at least in my experience working with low- and moderate-income families, but there is always work—and the harder we work, the more we win. The partnership with H&R Block has survived, though beaten about the head and face a bit, and with less money and enthusiasm perhaps, but still with a committed team on both sides, and it has made great strides. Change is never easy, and winning citizen wealth will be hard too.

Bernie? Ernst? They are still with us! They're now working for new organizations, but they're still in the same game! I think this proves my point. The citizen wealth bug is contagious. Once you catch it, you can't shake it.

We all need to spread this new citizen wealth gospel.

When we do that we will have the amazing experience of actually seeing something happen that changes the lives of lower-income and working families. The change in citizen wealth is one that keeps giving, generation after generation.

We really can do something about poverty. We really can create work with rewards and build families that have economic security.

We can stop talking about work as akin to a prison sentence and make it pay and provide citizen wealth all the way from the minimum wage to union scale.

When we heard that the poor will always be among us, this was not a promise or a guarantee so much as a prediction, and thus far, truth to tell, one that has found solid grounding in experience. But progress is being made here, and we can in fact make poverty a relative, rather than absolute, concept and change the meaning to refer to another citizen—an inhabitant of this great country—who simply has less wealth, rather than one who is abjectly poor.

We just need to get on with it, organize, and make it happen.

You take it from here to there.

Notes

Introduction: From the Bottom Up

1 Center on Budget and Policy Priorities, "Testimony of Robert Greenstein, Executive Director, Center on Budget and Policy Priorities," April 24, 2008, [Online] www.cbpp.org/4-24-08climate-testimony.pdf.

2 CBS News, "CBS Poll: 81% Say U.S. on Wrong Track," April 3, 2008, [Online] www.cbsnews.com/stories/2008/04/03/opinion/polls/main3992628.shtml.

3 ACORN International has membership organizations and affiliates in Canada, Peru, Mexico, Argentina, the Dominican Republic, India, and Kenya, with partnerships in Korea, Indonesia, the Philippines, and other countries.

4 CBS News, "The Rich Vs. the Filthy Rich," November 30, 2006, [Online] www.cbsnews.com/stories/2006/11/30/opinion/meyer/main2218369.shtml.

5 Urban Institute, "A Profile of Americans in Low-Income Working Families," October 1, 2000, [Online] www.urban.org/publications/309710.html.

6 Low-income working families receive fewer job benefits than middle-income families. Low-income families with at least one full-time worker are much less likely than middle-income families to receive health insurance through an employer (49 versus 77 percent): Urban Institute, "Low-Income Working Families: Facts and Figures," August 25, 2005, [Online] www.urban.org/publications/900832.html.

7 "Students from high-income families are five times more likely to enroll in college than their low-income peers. College-age black and Hispanic Americans are only about half as likely to be enrolled. Students who do go to college now leave with more than $19,000 in debt, twice as much as a decade ago": www.johnedwards.com/issues/education/college-for-everyone/.

8 Harvard Science, "Anatomy of the Low-Income Homeownership Boom in the 1990s," July 6, 2001, http://harvardscience.harvard.edu/culture-society/articles/anatomy-low-income-homeownership-boom-1990s; Randall S. Kroszner, "Mitigating the Impact of Foreclosures on Neighborhoods," May 7, 2008, www.federalreserve.gov/newsevents/speech/kroszner20080507a.htm.

9 Huliq, "Foreclosure Activity in USA Increased 75% in 2007," January 29, 2008, www.huliq.com/48701/foreclosure-activity-usa-increased-75-2007.

10 HUD, "Wealth Accumulation and Homeownership: Evidence for Low-Income Households," December 2004; http://ideas.repec.org/p/hud/wpaper/39045.html.

11 Robert B. Avery, Paul S. Calem, and Glenn B. Canner, "The Effects of the Community Reinvestment Act on Local Communities," paper presented at "Sustainable Community Development: What Works, What Doesn't and Why," a conference sponsored by the Board of Governors of the Federal Reserve System, March 27–28, 2003. Note: Research on the CRA has tended to find positive net effects, but the results are not uniform. A paper by board staff members compared census tracts just above and below the low- and moderate-income threshold, finding that the tracts below the threshold had higher home ownership rates, higher growth in owner-occupied units, and lower vacancy rates than would have otherwise been predicted.

12 See www.acorn.org/fileadmin/ACORN_Reports/2007/ACORN_Wins_Report.pdf.

13 "Athenian Democracy," www.wikipedia.com, accessed June 2007.

Chapter 1 Building a Winning Campaign for Economic Security

1 U.S. Census Bureau, "Selected Economic Characteristics, 2006 American Community Survey," May 27, 2008, [Online] http://factfinder.census.gov/servlet/ADPTable?_bm=y&-geo_id=01000US&-qr_name=ACS_2006_EST_G00_DP3&-ds_name=ACS_2006_EST_G00_&-_lang=en&-_sse=on.

2 United Nations Development Programme, *Human Development Report 2007/2008: Fighting Climate Change: Human Solidarity in a Changing World* (New York: Palgrave Macmillan 2007), [Online] http://hdr.undp.org/en/media/hdr_20072008_en_complete.pdf.

3 "Wal-Mart Business Profile," [Online] http://finance.yahoo.com/q/pr?s=WMT.

4 Thomas Shapiro, "The Hidden Cost of Being African American" (Washington, D.C.: Center for American Progress, February 1, 2004), [Online] www.americanprogress.org/issues/kfiles/b176427.html.

5 Gregory Squires, *Organizing Access to Capital: Advocacy and the Democratization of Financial Institutions* (Philadelphia: Temple University Press, 2003).

6 Michael Sherraden, *Inclusion in the American Dream: Assets, Poverty, and Public Policy* (New York: Oxford University Press, 2005).

7 Squires, *Organizing Access to Capital.*

8 Shapiro, "The Hidden Cost of Being African American."

9 Sherraden, *Inclusion in the American Dream.*

10 Lisa Keister, *Wealth in America: Trends in Wealth Inequality* (Cambridge: Cambridge University Press, 2000).

11 Javier Díaz-Giménez, Vincenzo Quadrini, and José-Víctor Ríos-Rull, "Dimensions of Inequality: Facts on the U.S. Distribution of Earnings, Income, and Wealth," *Federal Reserve Bank of Minneapolis Quarterly Review* 21, no. 2 (Spring 1997), p. 3.

12 Mark R. Rank, *One Nation, Underprivileged: Why American Poverty Affects Us All* (New York: Oxford University Press, 2004).

13 Shapiro, "The Hidden Cost of Being African American."

14 Ibid.

15 Ibid.

16 National Center for Health Statistics, "Early Release of Selected Estimates Based on Data from the 2007 National Health Interview Survey," June 25, 2008, [Online] www.cdc.gov/nchs/about/major/nhis/released200806.htm#1.

Chapter 2 Home Ownership Through Community Reinvestment

1 N. P. Retsinas and E. S. Belsky, *Low-Income Homeownership: Examining the Unexamined Goal* (Washington, D.C.: Brookings Institution Press, 2002), p. 201.
2 U.S. Department of Housing and Urban Development, "Economic Benefits of Increasing Minority Homeownership," 2002, p. 7, available at www.glensold.com/blueprint.pdf.
3 U.S. Federal Housing Administration 1938, par. 937, cited in *Revitalizing Urban Neighborhoods,* ed. W. Dennis Keating, Norman Krumholz, and Philip Star (Lawrence: University Press of Kansas, 1996), p. 223.
4 Ibid.
5 Dustin Mitchell, "Public Policy 246: The Community Reinvestment Act," University of Chicago, March 26, 2001, p. 6.
6 Ibid., p. 7.
7 Ibid.
8 Jim Campen, "The Community Reinvestment Act: A Law That Works," *Dollars and Sense* no. 214 (November 1997), p. 3.
9 Ibid.
10 HUD, "Economic Benefits of Increasing Minority Homeownership."
11 Gregory Squires, *Organizing Access to Capital: Advocacy and the Democratization of Financial Institutions* (Philadelphia: Temple University Press, 2003).
12 "The Performance and Profitability of CRA-Related Lending. Report by the Board of Governors of the Federal Reserve System, Submitted to the Congress Pursuant to Section 713 of the Gramm-Leach-Bliley Act of 1999" (Washington, D.C.: Federal Reserve System, 2000).
13 In 1984, the OCC only gave one rating worse than "satisfactory" to any of the 254 large banks they evaluated according: Mitchell, "Public Policy 246."
14 Ibid., p. 8.
15 Ibid., p. 9.
16 U.S. Census Bureau, American Housing Survey of 2001, [Online] www.census.gov/hhes/www/housing/ahs/ahs01/ahs01.html.
17 U.S. Census Bureau, American Housing Survey of 2003, [Online] www.census.gov/hhes/www/housing/ahs/ahs03/ahs03.html.
18 Thomas P. Boehm and Alan M. Schlottmann, "Housing and Wealth Accumulation: Intergenerational Impacts," Harvard University, Joint Center for Housing Studies, October 2001.
19 Andrew Schoenholtz and Kristin Stanton, *Reaching the Immigration Market and Creating Homeownership Opportunities for New Americans: A Strategic Business Planning Workbook* (Washington, D.C.: Fannie Mae Foundation and Georgetown University, 2001).
20 Lawrence K. Fish, "Economics of Immigration Reform," *Providence Journal,* April 30, 2006.
21 Steve Bergsman, "Banks Are Quietly Wooing Undocumented Immigrants," *U. S. Banker,* June 2005.

22 Ibid.

23 Ibid.

24 Carolyn Dicharry, "Money Under the Mattress: An Examination of Mexican Immigrants' Banking Habits in the U.S." (University of Oregon, June 2006). [Online] http://economics.uoregon.edu/honors/2006/banking.pdf.

Chapter 3 Stopping Foreclosures and Predatory Lending

1 Michael Dudley, "African American Homeownership Rates 'Falling Like a Rock,'" January 18, 2008, [Online] www.planetizen.com/node/29343.

2 "Predatory Lending," Arizona Attorney General's Office, Terry Goddard, Attorney General, July 2002.

3 Le mieux est l'ennemi du bien: The best is the enemy of the good: Voltaire, La Bégueule (1772).

4 Did this agreement provide the unions with much leverage? Having discussed the question with John Sweeney many times, I will not say none, but I can say, "Not so much."

5 Gene Hanson, "Homeowners Paying for Mortgage Woes," KC Community News, January 23, 2008.

6 Center for Responsible Lending, "Subprime Spillover," January 18, 2008.

7 Darryl Getter, "Understanding Mortgage Foreclosure: Recent Events, the Process, and Costs," November 5, 2007; [Online] http://assets.opencrs.com/rpts/RL34232_20071105.pdf.

8 Gerri Willis, "Protecting Your Home's Value," March 3, 2008, [Online] http://money.cnn.com/2008/03/03/pf/saving/toptips/index.htm?postversion=2008030312.

9 "Foreclosures Cost Lenders, Homeowners, the Community, and You Big Bucks," Mortgage News Daily, June 23, 2008.

10 Ibid.

11 Ibid.

Chapter 4 Making Work Pay Living Wages

1 "A Compilation of Living Wage Policies" (Washington, D.C.: ACORN Living Wage Resource Center, June 2006).

2 Laina Fox, "Indexing Minimum Wage for Inflation," December 21, 2005, [Online] www.epi.org/content.cfm/webfeatures_snapshots_20051221.

3 It was not until the last days of the first Clinton administration in 1996 that the minimum wage was increased.

4 Jon Gertner, "What Is a Living Wage?" New York Times Magazine, January 15, 2006.

5 Christopher Swope, "Living Wage Wars," December 1998, [Online] http://governing.com/archive/1998/dec/wage.txt.

6 Ron Ruggles, "Minimum Wage Hike Bills Springing Up Nationwide," February 3, 1997, [Online] http://findarticles.com/p/articles/mi_m3190/is_n5_v31/ai_19089490.

7 I should again disclose here that I am a founder of Local 100 and have been chief organizer of the local since its inception.

8 Amy Dean and Wade Rathke, "An Injury to One Is an Injury to All: Labor-Community Alliances and the New Labor Movement," New Labor Forum, September 29, 2008.

9 Proposition A of the 1996 Missouri General Election: no less than $6.25 as of January 1, 1997; $6.50 as of January 1, 1998; $6.75 as of January 1, 1999. 586,584 (28.7 percent) voted yes; 1,456,982 (71.3 percent) voted no: Office of the Secretary of State of Missouri.

10 Robert Pollin, Mark Brenner, and Jeannette Wicks-Lim, *Economic Analysis of the Florida Minimum Wage Proposal* (Washington, D.C.: Center for American Progress, Sept. 2004), [Online] www.americanprogress.org/atf/cf/%7BE9%20...%20E03%7D/minimumwage-layout8.pdf.

11 Estimate by Zach Polett, ACORN Political Department, on the 2006 elections.

12 This is a rough estimate, since the amount of time and effort spent by volunteeers and members is inestimable.

Chapter 5 Creating Wealth Through Worker Organizations

1 Andy Stern, *A Country That Works: Getting America Back on Track* (New York: Simon and Schuster, 2006.

2 U.S. Bureau of Labor Statistics, *Union Sourcebook 1947–1983.*

3 Ibid.

4 Leo Troy and Neil Sheflin, *Union Sourcebook: Membership, Finances, Structure, Directory* (West Orange, N.J.: Industrial Relations & Data, 1985).

5 Ibid.

6 BLS National Compensation Survey, July 2002.

7 Ibid.

8 Wade Rathke, "Labor's Failure in the South: A Key to the Puzzle," in Anthony Dunbar, ed., *American Crisis, Southern Solutions: From Where We Stand, Promise and Peril* (Montgomery, Ala.: New South Books, 2008).

9 *Seventy-First Annual Report of the NLRB for Fiscal Year Ended September 30, 2006* (Washington, D.C.: U.S. Government Printing Office, 2006).

10 John Schmitt and Ben Zipperer, "Dropping the Ax: Illegal Firings During Union Election Campaigns" (Washington, D.C.: Center for Economic and Policy Research, January 2007), [Online] www.cepr.net/documents/publications/unions_2007_01.pdf.

11 Ibid.

12 Ibid.

13 Meaning that union authorization cards might be tallied against an employee list and allow certification if a majority is demonstrated.

14 Shakespeare's King Richard III: "For fools rush in where angels fear to tread."

15 Key organizers from the ULU like Mark Splain, Keith Kelleher, Mike Gallagher, Peter Rider, Dale Ewart, Kirk Adams, Cecilie Richards, and others had long and important careers in the labor movement and elsewhere.

16 Under a successor company name, National, this first election victory and contract was brokered by Keith Kelleher and SEIU Local 880 into one of the few national organizing and collective agreements in all of SEIU.

17 Wade Rathke, "Majority Unionism: Strategies for Organizing the 21st-Century Labor Movement," *Social Policy* 35, no. 1 (Fall 2004), [Online] http://www.socialpolicy.org/index.php?id=1098.

18 The AARP (American Association of Retired Persons) is the largest organization in the United States with 35 million members who pay dues.

19 For Amicus's history, see the Amicus website, www.amicustheunion.org/default. aspx?page=9.

20 The other major paper presented in Seattle, by Stephen Lerner, argued for more "inside baseball": that the number of unions in the AFL-CIO needed to be shrunk, that unions needed to concentrate only on core jurisdictions, and that more resources needed to go into organizing, all of which became core arguments later in the break between SEIU and several other unions to form a new federation, Change to Win.

21 In the years between 2005–2008 WARN has blocked the development of thirty-four superstores.

22 The India FDI Watch Campaign focused on raising issues around the modification of foreign direct investment in retail in India (see www.indiafdiworld.org).

Chapter 6 Making Earned Income Tax Credits Work for Workers

1 Hilary W. Hoynes, "Presentation to the President's Advisory Panel on Federal Tax Reform," New Orleans, March 23, 2005; available at www.econ.ucdavis.edu/faculty/hoynes/presentations.html.

2 Ibid.

3 Ifie Okwuje and Nicholas Johnson, "A Rising Number of State Earned Income Tax Credits Are Helping Working Families Escape from Poverty" (Washington, D.C.: Center on Budget and Policy Priorities, October 20, 2006).

4 Hoynes, "Presentation," p. 2.

5 Ibid., p. 3.

6 Ibid.

7 Ibid., p. 5.

8 Ibid.

9 Ibid., p. 7.

10 Hilary W. Hoynes, Marianne E. Page, and Anne Huff Stevens, "Poverty in America: Trends and Explanations," June 9, 2005, [Online] www.npc.umich.edu/publications/workingpaper05/paper19/Poverty-6-9-05.pdf.

11 "EITC Boosts Local Economies," Federal Reserve Bank of Atlanta, vol. 16, no. 3, 2006.

12 Ibid.

13 Leonard E. Burman and Deborah Kobes, "EITC Reaches More Eligible Families Than TANF, Food Stamps" (Washington, D.C.: Urban Institute, March 17, 2003).

14 "Participation in the Earned Income Tax Credit Program Fiscal Year 2001 Research Project #12.26" (Fort Lauderdale/Greensboro: SE/SB Research, January 31, 2002), [Online] www.taxpolicycenter.org/TaxFacts/papers/irs_eitc.pdf.

15 U.C. Division of Agriculture and Natural Resources, "UC Study Finds Many Latinos Missing Out on Tax Credits," March 19, 2004, www.ucinthevalley.org/articles/2004/mar19art1.htm.

16 U.S. Internal Revenue Service, "Publication 596 (2007), Earned Income Credit (EIC)," [Online] www.irs.gov/publications/p596/index.html.

17 Henry J. Aaron and Joel Slemrod, The Crisis in Tax Administration (Washington, D.C.: Brookings Institution Press, 2004).

18 Statement of Leonard E. Burman before the United States House of Representatives Committee on the Budget: "On Waste, Fraud, and Abuse in Federal Mandatory Programs," July 9, 2003.

19 Thomas M. Shapiro and Edward N. Wolff, eds., *Assets for the Poor: The Benefits of Spreading Asset Ownership* (New York: Russell Sage Foundation, 2001).

20 Ibid.

21 Katherine S. Newman and Victor Tan Chen, *The Missing Class: Portraits of the Near Poor in America* (Boston: Beacon Press, 2007).

22 See Center for Social Development Washington University, "State IDA Policy Summary Tables," October 1, 2006, [Online] http://gwbweb.wustl.edu/csd/Policy/StateIDAtable.pdf.

23 For example, the Assets Policy Initiative of California represents a typically broad lineup; see www.assetpolicy-ca.org/.

23 Frances Fox Piven and Richard A. Cloward, "Northern Bourbons: A Preliminary Report on the National Voter Registration Act," *PS: Political Science & Politics 29*, no. 1 (March 1996): pp. 39–42.

25 Reports going into the 2008 presidential election indicated that we still have bigger problems with the machines than we do with the people, and of course with the people programming the machines!

26 Alan Berube, *Tienes EITC? A Study of the Earned Income Tax Credit in Immigrant Communities* (Washington, D.C.: Brookings Institution, April 2005), [Online] www.brookings.edu/reports/2005/04childrenfamilies_berube02.aspx.

27 Eduardo Porter, "Illegal Immigrants Are Bolstering Social Security with Billions," *New York Times*, April 5, 2005.

Chapter 7 Guarding Tax Refunds and Combatting High Prices

1 ACORN Financial Justice Center, "Increasing Incomes and Reducing the Rapid Refund Rip-Off" (St. Paul, Minn.: ACORN Financial Justice Center, 2004), [Online] www.caseygrants.org/documents/granteesinthenews/ACORN_report.pdf.

2 This was in fact the second prong in the strategy to deal with tax issues for lower-income families that was supported by the Marguerite Casey Foundation based on that lunchtime conversation and challenge.

3 Chi Chi Wu and Joan Anne Fox, "The NCLC/CFA 2008 Refund Anticipation Loan Report," March 2008, www.consumerfed.org/pdfs/RAL_2008_Report_final.pdf.

4 Lisa Donner, "ACORN Rips H&R Block 'Refund Anticipation Loans,'" January 23, 2004, [Online] www.acorn.org/index.php?id=1967&L=0%2Findex.php%253...#c4577.

5 Business Wire, "H&R Block Serves Record Total U.S. Clients in 2007 Tax Season," May 10, 2007, [Online] http://findarticles.com/p/articles/mi_m0EIN/is_2007_May_10/ai_n27233707.

6 ACORN Financial Justice Center, "Expanding Access to the Earned Income Tax Credit for Working Families While Reducing Reliance on Refund Anticipation Loans" (St. Paul, Minn.: ACORN Financial Justice Center, January 2007), [Online] http://acorn.org/fileadmin/ACORN_Reports/2007/EITC2007.pdf.

7 BBC News, "World Bank Tackles Food Emergency," April 14, 2008, [Online] http://news.bbc.co.uk/2/hi/business/7344892.stm.

8 Andre Vitchek, "Manufacturing Hunger: Report on Indonesia Food Crisis" (Oakland, Calif.: Oakland Institute, August 2008), www.asiananews.org.

9 Mark Nord, Margaret Andrews, and Steven Carlson, "Household Food Security in the United States, 2006" (Washington, D.C.: U.S. Department of Agriculture, November 2007), [Online] www.ers.usda.gov/publications/err49/.

10 H. Eric Schockman, "The Impact of Rising Food Prices on Low-Income Families in California: A Framework for the Federal and State Response." Testimony before the California State Assembly, May 15, 2008, p. 2.

11 Ibid.

12 Clifford Krauss, "Rural U.S. Takes Worst Hit as Gas Tops $4 Average," *New York Times*, June 9, 2008, www.nytimes.com/2008/06/09/business/09gas.html.

13 LIHEAP Fact Sheet, available online at www.liheap.org.

14 Eric Klineberg, *Heat Wave: A Social Autopsy of Disaster in Chicago* (Chicago: University of Chicago Press, 2002).

Chapter 8 The Debt Trap

1 Thomas P. Boehm and Alan M. Schlottmann, *Housing and Wealth Accumulation: Intergenerational Impacts* (Cambridge, Mass.: Harvard University, Joint Center for Housing Studies, October 2001), [Online] www.jchs.harvard.edu/publications/homeownership/liho01-15.pdf.

2 Alex Usher and Amy Cervenan, *Global Higher Education Report 2005: Affordability and Accessibility in Comparative Perspective* (Washington, D.C.: Educational Policy Institute, 2006), [Online] www.educationalpolicy.org/pdf/Global2005.pdf.

3 Ibid., p. iv.

4 Gretchen Morgensen, "The Debt Trap: Given a Shovel, Americans Dig Deeper into Debt," *New York Times*, July 20, 2008.

5 Javier Silva and Rebecca Epstein, *Costly Credit: African Americans and Latinos in Debt* (Washington, D.C.: Demos, 2005), [Online] http://archive.demos.org/pub529.cfm.

6 Ibid.

7 Ibid.

8 Ibid., p. 7.

9 Ibid.

10 Ibid., p. 6.

11 Ibid.

12 David Kraft and John Willis, *Survey of Payday Loan Users in Toronto and Vancouver* (Toronto: Canada ACORN, November 2005), [Online] www.acorn.org/fileadmin/International/Canada/Reports/stratcomm_payday_report.pdf.

13 Silva and Epstein, *Costly Credit*.

14 Austin King, ACORN Financial Justice Center.

15 "Ontario Meets ACORN's Key Demands with Payday Loan Legislation," Canada ACORN, [Online] www.acorn.org/index.php?id=16869.

16 John Kotter, "Alberta to Cap Interest Rates," *Edmonton Sun*, July 9, 2008.

17 Uriah King, Leslie Parrish, and Ozlem Tanik, *Financial Quicksand* (Durham, N.C.: Center for Responsible Lending, November 2006), [Online] www.responsiblelending.org/pdfs/rr012-Financial_Quicksand-1106.pdf.

18 Wade Rathke, "Momentum Overload," July 22, 2008, [Online] www.chieforganizer.org/index.php?id=57&no_cache=1&tx_eeblog%5BcategoryId%5D=19&tx_eeblog%5Bpointer%5D=0&tx_eeblog%5BshowUid%5D=26806.

19 Ben Bernanke, "Microfinance in the United States." Speech at the ACCIÓN Texas Summit on Microfinance in the United States, San Antonio, Texas, November 6, 2007, [Online] www.federalreserve.gov/newsevents/speech/bernanke20071106a.htm.

20 Miriam Jordan and Valerie Bauerlein, "Bank of America Casts Wider Net for Hispanics," *Wall Street Journal*, February 13, 2007.

21 Scarborough Research, "Unbanked Consumers: Unique Opportunities for Financial Marketers" (New York: Scarborough Research, March 2006, [Online] www. scarborough.com/press_releases/Unbanked%20Complimentary%20Report%20from %20Scarborough%20FINAL%203.16.06%20A.pdf .

22 For more on this coalition, see www.transnationalaction.org.

Chapter 9 The "Maximum Eligible Participation" Solution

1 Richard W. Boone, "Special Issue: Citizens Action in Model Cities and CAP Programs: Case Studies and Evaluation," *Public Administration Review* 32 (Sept. 1972), pp. 444–56.

2 Now officially called the Supplemental Nutrition Assistance Program (SNAP).

3 Richard Cloward and Frances Piven, "The Weight of the Poor: A Strategy to End Poverty," *Nation*, May 2, 1966.

4 I was an organizer for MWRO, first in Springfield, where a campaign to win winter clothing for adults taught me many life lessons about power, and then as head organizer of MWRO based in Boston after Pastreich took another assignment.

5 Dues in NWRO were $1.00 per year, if they were collected at all.

6 Food Research & Action Council (FRAC), March 2008 Bulletin.

7 Ibid.

8 Liz Wolff, ACORN Research Report, January, 2008.

9 U.S. Department of Agriculture Food and Nutrition Service, Food and Nutrition Service Research & Evaluation Plan—Fiscal Year 2008, September 2007, [Online] http://www.fns.usda.gov/oane/MENU/Published/Research/FY2008RandE.pdf.

10 We are encouraged, though, by the Half in Ten Campaign, sponsored by four organizations (the Center for American Progress Action Fund, the Leadership Conference on Civil Rights, Coalition on Human Needs, and ACORN), which has announced a goal of reducing the poverty rate by half over the next ten years.

11 Wayne Vroman, *An Introduction to Unemployment and Unemployment Insurance* (Washington, D.C.: Urban Institute, October 2005), [Online] www.urban.org/ UploadedPDF/311257_unemployment.pdf.

12 Ibid.

13 Ibid.

14 Ibid., p. 2.

15 Cloward and Piven, "The Weight of the Poor."

Chapter 10 Working with Corporations to Create an Asset Climate

1 A famous line from Bob Dylan's "Subterranean Homesick Blues" of 1965.

2 "Fortune Global 500 Financial Institutions," [Online] http://money.cnn.com/ magazines/fortune/global500/2007/snapshots/7597.html.

3 Mark McQueen, "HSBC to Discontinue Off-Season Tax Refund Lending," March 18, 2007, [Online] http://seekingalpha.com/article/29873-hsbc-to-discontinue-off-season-tax-refund-lending.

4 Internal Revenue Bulletin 2008-5, [Online] www.irs.gov/irb/2008-05_IRB/index.html.

Chapter 11 Business Models That Foster Citizen Wealth

1 A Citibank term that I find fascinating.

2 A story I was never able to confirm or deny.

3 ACORN, WARN, Wal-Mart Watch, and others did oppose a similar initiative by Wal-Mart to get an industrial bank charter in Utah, where it had initially been unwilling to agree to CRA standards.

4 Of course this business model was quickly proven wrong, since the banking meltdown of 2008 has shown that without a huge deposit base, such as Bank of America has, a major financial institution cannot survive. Investment banks have been rechartered as bank holding companies, and access to retail customers and the acquisition of banks with a diverse stream of such deposits is the new model in the U.S. Citi is now madly trying to fashion a way to survive, having failed to acquire Wachovia in a competition with Wells Fargo, and is trying to find other ports in the storm to shore up its balance sheet with more deposits.

5 Wal-Mart Watch, *Low Prices at What Cost?: Wal-Mart Watch's 2005 Annual Report* (Washington, D.C.: Wal-Mart Watch/Center for Community & Corporate Ethics, 2005), [Online] http://walmartwatch.com/research/documents/low_prices_at_what_cost_wal_mart_watchs_2005_annual_report/.

6 Wikipedia: "Wal-Mart," [Online] 2008 http://en.wikipedia.org/wiki/Wal-Mart.

7 Ibid.

8 Fortune Global 500 (2008), [Online] http://money.cnn.com/magazines/fortune/global500/2008/full_list/.

9 Walmart Stores International Division, 2008, [Online] http://walmartstores.com/AboutUs/246.aspx.

10 William M. Bulkeley, "'Category Killers' Look Vulnerable, Not Deadly," *Wall Street Journal*, March 9, 2000.

11 Jason Furman, "Wal-Mart: A Progressive Success Story," November 28, 2005, [Online] http://www.americanprogress.org/kf/walmart_progressive.pdf.

12 Ibid.

13 Jerry Hausman and Ephraim Leibtag, "Consumer Benefits from Increased Competition in Shopping Outlets: Measuring the Effect of Wal-Mart." Presentation at the EC2 Conference, December 2004, [Online] http://www.globalinsight.com/publicDownload/genericContent/hausman.pdf.

14 Furman, "Wal-Mart: A Progressive Success Story."

15 Ibid.

16 U.S. Bureau of Labor Statistics, "Union Affiliation of Employed Wage and Salary Workers by Occupation and Industry," January 25, 2008, [Online] www.bls.gov/news.release/union2.t03.htm.

17 Furman, "Wal-Mart: A Progressive Success Story."

18 Arindrajit Dube, Dave Graham-Squire, Ken Jacobs, and Stephanie Luce, "Living Wage Policies and Wal-Mart," [Online] MRZine: www.monthlyreview.org/mrzine/walmart101207.html.

19 WARN, "Wal-Mart Real Wage and Turnover Study," November 2006, [Online] http://
    www.aflcio.org/corporatewatch/walmart/upload/walmart_wagestudy_fla.pdf.

20 Ibid.

21 *Dukes v. Wal-Mart*, Case No 04-16688 (9th Cir. Feb. 6, 2007); see Michael S. Kun,
    "What the Historic *Dukes v. Wal-Mart* Decision Means for Employers," Metropolitan
    Corporate Counsel, [Online] www.metrocorpcounsel.com/current.php?artType=vie
    w&artMonth=March&artYear=2007&EntryNo=6353.

22 Amaris Elliott-Engel, "Philadelphia Judge Awards Wal-Mart Workers $62M More,"
    October 4, 2007, [Online] www.law.com/jsp/article.jsp?id=900005557684.

23 Wal-Mart Watch, *Wal-Mart: Save Money or Bust Unions* (Washington, D.C.: Wal-
    Mart Watch/Center for Community & Corporate Ethics, 2005), [Online] http://
    walmartwatch.com/img/documents/walmart_unions.pdf.

24 Michael Barbaro, "Wal-Mart Chief Defends Closing Unionized Store," *Washington
    Post*, February 11, 2005.

25 I should offer a personal disclosure at this point. I founded the WARN project and have
    directed its work along with Rick Smith in Florida, Texas, and California for the last
    several years. At the same time I was quoted several years ago (Katrina vanden Heuvel,
    "Sweet Victory: Celebrating ACORN") in the *Nation* (September 13, 2005) saying as
    a customer and seven-and-a-half-year former Arkansas resident, "I love that store," so
    the reader will have to balance all of that out for herself.

26 See www.AARP.com.

27 Eric Schurenberg and Lani Luciano, "The Empire Called AARP," *Money*, October 1,
    1988.

28 AARP Annual Report, available at www.AARP.com.

29 CBS News, "Jamie Lee Curtis Strips Down for AARP," March 21, 2008, [Online]
    http://www.cbsnews.com/stories/2008/03/21/entertainment/main3958872.shtml.

30 For AARP's membership terms, see www.aarp.org/membership/aarp/a2003-09-09-
    conditions_membership.html.

31 Universal Health Services, Inc., http://appsrv2.uhsinc.com/Apps/HR/JobPosting.
    nsf/AARP?OpenPage.

32 Nicolas Paul Retsinas and Eric S. Belsky, *Low-Income Homeownership: Examining the
    Unexamined Goal* (Washington, D.C.: Brookings Institution Press, 2002).

33 Center for Financial Services Innovation (CFSI), "Marrying Financial Transactions with
    Asset-Building Opportunities" (Chicago: Center for Financial Services Innovation, July
    2005).

34 Ibid., p. 3.

35 Ibid., p. 4.

36 Ibid.

37 Federal Reserve Bank of New York, 2004, quoted in CFSI, "Marrying Financial
    Transactions."

38 See www.netspend.com.

39 Ibid., p. 6.

40 Jay Rosenstein, ed., "Special Edition: 51 Ways to Save Hundreds on Loans and Credit
    Cards," *FDIC Bulletin* (Summer 2007), [Online] www.fdic.gov/consumers/consumer/
    news/cnsum07/index.html.

41 Ibid.

42 Ibid.

43 Ibid.

44 This is a real opportunity for community groups and programs like the ACORN Centers!
45 Ibid., p. 3.
46 Ibid., p. 7.

Chapter 12 Bringing Citizens into the Wealth-Building Process

1 Family Strengthening Policy Center, *Community Health Workers: Closing Gaps in Families' Health Resources* (Washington, D.C.: Family Strengthening Center, July 2005), [Online] www.nydic.org/fspc/practice/documents/Brief14.pdf.
2 Center on Budget and Policy Priorities, *Food Stamps Online: A Review of State Government Food Stamp Websites* (Washington, D.C.: Center on Budget and Policy Priorities, 2005, [Online] www.cbpp.org/8-25-03fa.pdf.
3 Ibid.
4 According to Diné Butler, national coordinator for the ACORN National Centers, six new electronic submission centers were approved in 2008, located in Wisconsin, Delaware, Kansas, California, Washington, and New Jersey.
5 Another lesson that should remind all citizens that we need a citizen-centered government.
6 S. G. Beverly, J. L. Romich, and J. Tescher, "Linking Tax Refunds and Low-Cost Bank Accounts: A Social Development Strategy for Low-Income Families?" *Social Development Issues* 25, nos. 1/2 (2004), pp. 235–46.
7 "H&R Blockbuster," *New York Times*, May 17, 2005.
8 Hilary Johnson, "Underbanked: H&R Block's Emerald Card Wins Customers," Center for Financial Services Innovation/ShoreBank, May 12, 2008, [Online] http://www.cfsinnovation.com/in_the_news_archive-detail.php?article_id=330352.

Chapter 13 The Future of Citizen Wealth

1 Lillian Woo and David Buchholz, *Return on Investment? Getting More from Federal Asset-Building Policies* (Washington, D.C.: CFED, 2006).
2 Ibid., p. 6.
3 Ibid., p. 3.
4 Ibid.
5 Ibid.
6 U.S. Department of Health and Human Services, "Assets for Independence Program Study" [Online] http://www.acf.hhs.gov/programs/ocs/afi/fact_sheet.html.
7 Ibid., p. 5.
8 Ibid., p. 6.
9 Ibid., p. 7.
10 The minimum wage at the time was still $5.15 per hour.
11 Urban Institute, *Government Work Supports and Low-Income Families: Fact and Figures* (Washington, D.C.: Urban Institute, July 2006).
12 Ibid., p. 2.
13 Lillian Woo and David Buchholz, *Getting More from Federal Asset Building Policies* (Washington, D.C.: CFED, 2007), [Online] http://www.cfed.org/imageManager/_documents/publications/hips2/return_on_investment.pdf.

Acknowledgments

Props to many and thanks to all!

When you build an organization, by definition from the first meeting it ceases to be about the organizer and becomes about the many who make it live and grow and win. None of this book could have been written, or would have been worth reading, without the sacrifice and struggle of literally thousands of grassroots leaders and members who have swelled the ranks of the organizations that I have been honored to serve over the last more than forty years. In that sense anything right about this book is to their credit and anything wrong about it should rightfully stick to the bottom of my boots.

Specifically, let me single out the presidents of the ACORN board during my tenure as chief organizer, because they are my personal heroes and in a thousand ways have led the organization grandly for the last dozen or more years: Steve McDonald (Little Rock), Larry Rodgers (Little Rock), Elena Hanggi Giddings (Little Rock), Mildred Brown (Philadelphia), and, especially, Maude Hurd (Boston). They have written new definitions for the meaning of community leadership. I would say the same for the great presidents of Local 100 SEIU where I have also served as chief organizer, Mildred Edmond and then Rebecca Hart of New Orleans and Sedric Crawford and Vernon Bolden of Baton Rouge. They have all been warriors for workers! Best for me, all of them have taught me patience, since I have little, and shown me patience when I must have been most trying. I know reading the book will remind all of them still living of the many battles we have shared along with the defeats and victories that have forged our futures together.

Let me honor a couple of other people who took chances with me that made a difference. George Wiley, now long deceased, founded and directed the National Welfare Rights Organization, and was willing to see the potential in a young, redheaded kid and backed me all the way on my crazy vision for building ACORN, as long as he could. John Sweeney, now president of the AFL-CIO, and Andy Stern, first as organizing director of SEIU and then as president of SEIU, did the same in letting me build Local 100 as a premier union of lower-income workers in the South and organize hotel workers in New Orleans and Wal-Mart workers in Florida using different ways and means that others would never have allowed. Drummond Pike, the founder of the Tides network of philanthropic organizations in San Francisco, has been a constant funder of my wild ideas, both big and small, over the last thirty-five years, so it was a pleasure to serve with the small favors I could provide as a member of the Tides board for thirty-two of those years, and an even greater honor to call him a friend throughout this period.

I cannot thank all of the organizers by name who have worked with me over the years, but I know I have told all of them that their time as organizers would be that gift that is as good as it gets in life, and I know that has been the same for me. All of you were great. I just wish I could have been even better to lead you further, but every win in this book and in the future is also yours to savor for the time you spent and the work you did.

Thanks to the three directors of the ACORN Financial Justice Center, Lisa Donner, Jordan Ash, and Austin King, particularly for their work with me on the campaigns around predatory practices with subprime mortgages and tax preparers. Thanks to Mike Shea with ACORN Housing, who was my partner in many tough negotiations with some of these banks. I cannot leave Helene O'Brien out, who made the trains run on time as ACORN's field director during the last decade of my work with ACORN. Jeff Karlson and Diné Butler have done amazing work in building the ACORN Centers and, if they had the support and resources, could prove that "maximum eligible participation" actually works.

On the other side of the table, it gives me real hope to find that there are still people like Eric Eve at Citi and Stuart Tait at HSBC, that Bernie Wilson was such a mensch at H&R Block, and that people like Marc Ferguson at Nets 2 Ladders and Trooper Sanders, formerly of the Clinton Foundation, really get what we have to do to build citizen wealth. There are more people than I ever would have expected who deserve applause and a shout-out than I have space for in these pages, but this thanks is for you as well. I know how hard it is for you to survive in your companies these days, so I'm going to do you the favor of not thanking you by name, and we will leave it at that.

Sometimes I have perhaps more discipline than good sense, so that when I hunkered down to write this book, I needed to get it done. My family, despite there not being a liberal among them, let me write the outline for this book from Lisbon, Portugal, on their time during Christmas 2007, and then also while I was writing the first big chunk of this on a busman's holiday we took to Gulf Shores, Alabama, in late July 2008. I have dedicated the book to them for good reason. My mother, Cornelia Ratliff Rathke, was with us that week, and both of us probably were thinking way too much of my father, Edmann Jacob Rathke, who had suddenly passed away in June, but having her with us and having him in my mind helped me put my shoulder to the wheel. Both of my parents, when they agreed with my work and when they disagreed with it strenuously, have nonetheless supported me on this great quest uncategorically. It is hard to ask for more or to thank them enough. I finally got this book done thanks to the support and good grace of Ercilia Sahores, director of ACORN International's Latin American operations, who protected my writing time every morning from her apartment in Buenos Aires for two weeks in Agosto, and organized my time with her staff and members for the afternoons. *Muchas gracias*, Ercilia!

Johanna Vondeling has been my editor at Berrett-Koehler. She searched me out and convinced me that I should write a book with B-K and then kept with me until we got it done with a soft sell and steady, strong support. For me this was all an education and she and her colleagues at B-K could not have been better to me as a newbie author. Furthermore, Johanna and her crew are people of conviction and character, and in the dustups of the summer of 2008 and the wildness of the political campaign and so much else, if they ever wavered,

I would not have known it, because their support for me and this project was profound and unstinting.

Thanks to Shaena Johnson for all of her research assistance on this book and to Nicole Washington, who has organized a lot of my life to enable me to get so many things done.

Finally, thanks to Barack Obama and Sarah Palin for proving past my wildest imagination how important organizing and organizers are, and how much responsibility we all have for making the world not just different, but better.

Index

About the Author

Wade Rathke first began organizing more than forty years ago when he dropped out of college to organize against the Vietnam War. Later he organized welfare recipients in Massachusetts, first in Springfield and then statewide from Boston, before leaving for Arkansas to found ACORN in Little Rock in mid-June 1970. A decade later, Wade added labor organizing to his experiences when he and other organizers responded to issues that ACORN members were having in their workplaces, whether home health workers, hotel workers, or fast food workers, and moved to New Orleans to build independent unions that later merged into the Service Employees International Union in 1984.

The common themes of these decades as a welfare rights organizer, community organizer, and labor organizer have been how to unite people at the bottom income levels around their issues to build sufficient power so that they could impact their lives, improve their communities, and change the direction of their country. Dealing with income and assets has been a constant theme of Wade's organizing, no matter what the venue or vehicle, and he has been delighted to pull all of these strands of his experience together in writing *Citizen Wealth*. For a generation Wade has been recognized as perhaps the premier organizer of his generation, making this book something of a milestone in that journey.

Wade left ACORN after thirty-eight years as its chief organizer in mid-2008, when the organization had more than 100 offices and close to 500,000 members. Now he continues as chief organizer of ACORN International, working in Canada, Mexico, Peru, Argentina, the Dominican Republic, India, and Kenya, and with partnerships in Indonesia, Korea, and the Philippines. Once again he is working to assist in building membership-based organizations largely in the mega-slums of Dharavi (Mumbai), La Matanza (Buenos Aires), NEZA (Mexico City), and San Juan Laraguache (Lima) that have arisen in some of the world's largest cities. ACORN International is also organizing unions of hawkers and wastepickers in Delhi and Mumbai and *cartoneros* in Buenos Aires.

In the United States Wade continues to serve as chief organizer of Local 100, Service Employees International Union, headquartered in New Orleans, with members in Louisiana, Arkansas, and Texas. He also directs a campaign to make Wal-Mart accountable to its workers and communities in Florida, California, and India.

In recent years Wade has had the opportunity to learn more about other organizing around America and the rest of the world as chair of the Organizers' Forum, which once a year looks at common problems for community and labor organizers, and once a year travels to other countries to learn about the challenges and experiences of organizations elsewhere. Thus far he has led delegations of organizers to Brazil, India, South Africa, Indonesia, Turkey, Russia, and Australia. Having been a board member for thirty-two years (and now senior adviser) of the San Francisco–based Tides family of philanthropic enterprises, he has had the opportunity in that capacity to support the incubation of many campaigns and organizations housed with the Tides Center or funded by the Tides Foundation. Similarly, as publisher and editor-in-chief of *Social Policy* magazine, he has been able to offer a forum for the many voices from organizing, academia, and elsewhere on issues that matter around social change here and abroad.

Living and working in New Orleans, where ACORN had its headquarters during the destruction wrought by Hurricane Katrina in 2005, Wade and the entire ACORN family were intimately involved in the fight to rebuild the city, especially the lower-income areas like the 9th Ward, where ACORN members were concentrated. Wade remarks that now he could not leave the city, even if he wanted to, because fighting to come back from Katrina made it home for everyone who shared this experience no matter where they were born (Wyoming in Wade's case) or how long they had been here. (To support the recovery work still very much going on, go to www. hurricaneoutreach.org.)

Wade's partner, Beth Butler, is also a longtime community organizer and executive director of Louisiana ACORN. Their two children, Chaco Butler Rathke and Diné Rathke Butler, were born and raised in New Orleans and have now returned to the city to do their part in its recovery and to work for the same causes that have defined the family forever.

Wade is easy to find. Calls are not screened and the door is always open if you are on Elysian Fields and he happens to be in town. Always follow the work first, and that can be done through www.acorninternational.org. When looking for Wade, the easiest is to check out his website at www.waderathke.org or his blog at www.chieforganizer. org and see where he is and what he is up to.

And if you want to help build the campaign to create citizen wealth, join with others at www.citizenwealth.org.

About Berrett-Koehler Publishers

Berrett-Koehler is an independent publisher dedicated to an ambitious mission: Creating a World That Works for All.

We believe that to truly create a better world, action is needed at all levels—individual, organizational, and societal. At the individual level, our publications help people align their lives with their values and with their aspirations for a better world. At the organizational level, our publications promote progressive leadership and management practices, socially responsible approaches to business, and humane and effective organizations. At the societal level, our publications advance social and economic justice, shared prosperity, sustainability, and new solutions to national and global issues.

A major theme of our publications is "Opening Up New Space." They challenge conventional thinking, introduce new ideas, and foster positive change. Their common quest is changing the underlying beliefs, mindsets, and structures that keep generating the same cycles of problems, no matter who our leaders are or what improvement programs we adopt.

We strive to practice what we preach—to operate our publishing company in line with the ideas in our books. At the core of our approach is *stewardship*, which we define as a deep sense of responsibility to administer the company for the benefit of all of our "stakeholder" groups: authors, customers, employees, investors, service providers, and the communities and environment around us.

We are grateful to the thousands of readers, authors, and other friends of the company who consider themselves to be part of the "BK Community." We hope that you, too, will join us in our mission.

A BK Currents Book

This book is part of our BK Currents series. BK Currents books advance social and economic justice by exploring the critical intersections between business and society. Offering a unique combination of thoughtful analysis and progressive alternatives, BK Currents books promote positive change at the national and global levels. To find out more, visit www.bkcurrents.com.

Be Connected

Visit Our Website

Go to www.bkconnection.com to read exclusive previews and excerpts of new books, find detailed information on all Berrett-Koehler titles and authors, browse subject-area libraries of books, and get special discounts.

Subscribe to Our Free E-Newsletter

Be the first to hear about new publications, special discount offers, exclusive articles, news about bestsellers, and more! Get on the list for our free e-newsletter by going to www.bkconnection.com.

Get Quantity Discounts

Berrett-Koehler books are available at quantity discounts for orders of ten or more copies. Please call us toll-free at (800) 929-2929 or email us at bkp.orders@aidcvt.com.

Host a Reading Group

For tips on how to form and carry on a book reading group in your workplace or community, see our website at www.bkconnection.com.

Join the BK Community

Thousands of readers of our books have become part of the "BK Community" by participating in events featuring our authors, reviewing draft manuscripts of forthcoming books, spreading the word about their favorite books, and supporting our publishing program in other ways. If you would like to join the BK Community, please contact us at bkcommunity@bkpub.com.